Your Ernst, Who Is Always Faithful to You

LETTERS FROM ANOTHER TIME

STEVEN ROESCH

authorHOUSE®

AuthorHouse™
1663 Liberty Drive
Bloomington, IN 47403
www.authorhouse.com
Phone: 1 (800) 839-8640

Published by AuthorHouse 11/11/2019

ISBN: 978-1-7283-3380-9 (sc)
ISBN: 978-1-7283-3379-3 (hc)
ISBN: 978-1-7283-3378-6 (e)

Library of Congress Control Number: 2019917346

Print information available on the last page.

DEDICATION

This book is dedicated my parents, who—in their quiet, unassuming way—both lived remarkable lives.

PREFACE

*A*t first glance they hardly looked very impressive at all.

They were a set of chocolate-brown accordion files, and we found them on the top shelf of the entrance closet. Each file bulged with scores of letters, postcards, and documents that hailed from the years 1945 to 1952, and every single item had been carefully preserved in a clear plastic sheath. Some included comments in German that our mother had written on them. A good number had clearly been censored here and there; instead of a full page of writing, for example, the top or bottom half of a page had been neatly clipped off now and then.

My brother Thomas and I came across them while we were going through our childhood home in May 2016, and at the time we just set them aside. We had a lot to sort through and pack up, and there was precious little time to complete our task.

Both of us already had a general idea of what those letters and documents were about. We knew the general outlines of our parents' early history, though not too much. Amalie Roesch, our grandmother, had been Jewish, and she'd been sent to a concentration camp during World War II. Our father, Ernst Roesch, had been considered a half-Jew and sent to a labor camp during that time. Both survived, and shortly thereafter both emigrated to the United States, where they settled in Lodi, California. At some point Ernst began writing to our mother—Liselotte Peschel, as she was called back then. They'd known each other earlier on, and their friendship now continued as she sent him letters of her own on occasion.

Things took an unexpected turn when our father got a draft notice from the U.S. government. After completing basic training, he was assigned to a post in Berlin. Now, at long last, he could see her again in person. Their courtship led to engagement, to their wedding in the fall of 1952, and finally to the family constellation that we knew and took for granted.

We'd heard about these letters before, usually from our mother. Sometimes, caught up in a cloud of nostalgia, our dad would withdraw and read through some of them to recapture the spirit and magic of those earlier times. Beyond that, we knew very little, and we certainly never expected so many of them, nor did we know what was in them, exactly.

After Tom and I wrapped up our work in the house, I brought the accordion files back with me to my home in Fresno. For a while they just sat in one of my filing cabinets, neglected the way they'd been for years—or at least since 2014, when our mother had passed.

Being retired, I had ample time to work my way through all of them, and when I got around to looking at them, I quickly realized how valuable they were. I'm not sure when I decided to begin translating them, but once I started it became part of my daily routine. My original motive was a simple one. Our parents, as well as all of our grandparents, were now deceased; Ursula, my older sister, had also passed. I wanted my two remaining siblings, Thomas and Barbara, to be able to read and appreciate this correspondence. Although both could speak and understand some German, neither had the skill to get through these letters. Rebecca, Tom's wife, couldn't read them in their original form, either; nor could their two children, Walter and Mattie. Everyone in the family deserved to be privy to their content, given the wealth of information that they contained.

Initially I figured that putting them into English would be a slam dunk. I'd majored in German and English at the University of the Pacific and later done graduate work in Comparative Literature at the University of Toronto. I'd also just finished a thirty-year stint teaching German and English. In the Eighties I'd translated some scholarly essays for publication—texts that had dealt with sociology and psychoanalysis. In theory, then, rendering my parents' words in English couldn't be all that challenging.

Unexpected problems and hurdles came my way, though. The handwriting, for one thing. I couldn't decipher some of the earlier missives at all, and I needed to find others to help me figure out how certain individual letters were being formed.

Beyond the handwriting, some of the letters that my dad had typed proved to be a vexing problem as well. Typing didn't come easily for him, and it showed.

After a few months my project was complete. I put English versions of our parents' letters into chronological order and copied them onto two flash drives—one for Tom and one for Barbara. I also scanned the pictures and documents from our parents' photo albums and included these on the flash drives.

Except the project didn't feel complete at all. The missives that our parents had written almost always touched on a spectrum of topics, usually with a scattershot approach to organization. Just reading through the letters in order seemed to obscure and conceal their personalities rather than illuminate them. You could easily get lost in a bewildering maze of details and lose sight of the larger narrative of their lives.

Almost all of them opened and ended with conventional, fairly predictable phrases. *Last Friday I received your letter of September 23, 1947. Thanks so much!* is the way that our mother began her letter of October 5, 1947, for example. Perusing these sections wasn't all that engaging, nor did it provide much insight into the people who wrote them.

All of the colorful and intriguing nuggets of new information were scattered elsewhere, beyond these conventional phrases and niceties. It just didn't seem fair to leave things this way—to be satisfied with English translations of the raw letters. My relatives needed more than this.

Then it hit me. I could organize these materials according to various topics and convey our parents' story that way. Sure, some portions of the original letters wouldn't be included in these new categories, but overall this approach would give members of my family a better understanding of the young Ernst Roesch and Liselotte Peschel. The results wouldn't exactly be chronological anymore, but they would offer a far more vivid and informative portrait of my parents.

I came up with a set of categories that seemed to work—Education and Hardships, for example—and then printed out the entire set of letters and began marking them up according to which parts could be assigned to which category. I noticed that my father had written extensively about his adventures—and occasional mishaps—in the Sierra Nevadas. My mother, for her part, also relished hikes in the great outdoors, not to mention parties during Munich's annual *Fasching* celebrations. And so another category was born—Leisure. It seemed natural and necessary to make the final category Love—a chapter that would focus on their developing relationship, one which would blossom after my father found himself wearing a U.S. army uniform and stationed in Berlin in 1951.

And that could have been the end of the project. But then something else happened.

In September 2017 I began doing volunteer work at Manchester GATE, a local elementary school—although calling this "work" is a stretch. Two teachers, Richard Vezzolini and Karen Barretto, ran a chess program there, and I dropped by every Thursday afternoon to help them prepare their students for occasional tournaments. Once, in 2018, I got to Richard's classroom early and noticed that his class had been reading about the Holocaust. I took Richard aside, let him know about my family history, and asked if I could share my story with his students. A few weeks later he invited me over to his classroom, and over the months that followed several of his colleagues asked me to give similar presentations for their classes. Their graciousness and the positive response of their students inspired me to go one step further and turn my translated material into this book. Needless to say, I'm now continuing to speak to students about my parents from time to time.

All of the translations included here—including sections of the Hesse poem and the Lehar opera libretto—are my own.

Although I've gathered my own collection of correspondence over the years, few of my friends' letters are as lengthy and detailed as the ones that my parents wrote. The letters in my own accordion files are usually a mere one or two pages long. And today, as a rule, we tend to communicate tersely, using emails or social media. We all tend to eschew handwriting in favor of texting and word processing.

Ernst Roesch and Liselotte Peschel belonged to another generation, though, one which often left a far more substantial epistolary footprint—a footprint so palpable that many times, as I worked my way through their words, I could hear their voices again and see their faces. Their letters have given me a keyhole of sorts that I can use to peer into another time, one with a different rhythm and decidedly different social conventions. They often ended their letters with phrases like "With affection" and "With love," and many times they underlined these words to emphasize that their sentiments were real and heartfelt—not mere stock phrases. Thinking about that now, I realize that love and affection also prompted and fueled this project of mine over the past few years.

CHAPTER ONE

Fog

No one knows anyone else. Everyone is alone.

It's strange to roam through the fog.
Every bush and every stone is isolated.
No tree sees another—
Each one is alone.

So goes the first stanza of Hermann Hesse's *Im Nebel*—"In the Fog." He concludes his poem by observing that an existential fog pervades our lives, one that quietly and consistently separates each of us from everyone else. As a result, *"No one knows anyone else"* and *"Each of us is alone."*

Part of me has always been drawn to these lines because of the atmosphere they evoke. Hesse's words remind me of a time in the mid-Seventies when I studied at the state university in Freiburg im Breisgau in what was, back then, West Germany. On many mornings when I walked from my dorm to the Littenweiler streetcar stop, I could spot wispy fingers of fog reaching up from the treetops in the Black Forest. Hesse's verse still comes to mind whenever I edge through the dense and sometimes dangerous tule fog in California's Central Valley. On another level *Im Nebel* has served as a sage admonishment for me—that, despite my best efforts, those around me will always be, in a very real and inevitable sense, beyond the reach of my understanding. I'll always only be able to grasp a part of their nature, just a segment of their true and complete selves. I've realized this again and again when it comes to colleagues at my school, to my students and neighbors, and of course to more ephemeral acquaintances that I've met during my travels.

Somehow, though, it took me a lot longer to figure out that Hesse's lament also applies to members of my immediate family—and, specifically, to my own parents.

The students admired the way that I was so calm about it...

On January 24, 1980, an earthquake hit central California with a vengeance, measuring 5.5 on the Richter scale. It focused its fury on Livermore and Stockton, but Lodi—my home town, about twelve miles north of Stockton—was also impacted. Back then I was a graduate student at the University of Toronto; my parents were both still living in Lodi, where my mother had a part-time job managing the library at St. Anne's School. That evening, with the memory of the earthquake fresh in her mind, she sat down and wrote to me in German—as she always did—about what had transpired during those nerve-wracking moments.

As it turned out, she was hosting a group of fourth-graders when the quake struck.

When it hit, my students were standing along the bookshelves and on chairs to reach the upper shelves. It was the fourth-grade class. I tried to keep everyone calm; I let all of them sit down right away. One girl—a Japanese girl—almost got sick. If it had gone on longer, we would have sought protection under the big table. It was as if a strong force was surging through the room like a large, powerful wave on the high seas. The students admired the way that I was so calm about it, and they thought that I'd had experience with earthquakes before. I told them that I'd never been in an earthquake before—but I'd been in air raids! When everything settled down, I told them that we should say a prayer. That way I could keep them quiet and still for a while longer. I kept reminding them to stay that way; staying calm is the most important thing. Our bookshelves swayed, and the books slid a bit. Everything went well!

My mother's reaction to the earthquake—as well as her allusion to the air raids she'd lived through—gave me a small glimpse into the life she'd led during World War II. In moments like this one a gap opened in the metaphorical fog that Hesse had written about, helping me to sense something about her earlier trials and the strength and resolve that she'd garnered during those difficult times.

"With Understanding"

Something similar happened years ago that gave me a better sense of my father—the person beyond the "dad" that all four of us children interacted with every day.

One day in the 1960s, when we were on summer vacation in the Sierras, we sat around a picnic table and feasted on sandwiches and soft drinks. Around us the pine trees loomed like wise observers, and we could bask in the distinct scent of pine needles wafting in our direction.

Out of the blue our father told us about how he used to make sandwiches for himself when he was a boy. He'd put a truncated sliver of salami on top of a single piece of bread, placing it at the far end so that he could see it as he started munching on the opposite side. That way, he let us know with a shrewd twinkle in his eyes, you could fool yourself. Looking at the meat—but only munching on bread for a while—you could convince yourself that you were actually already tasting salami as well. In times when food was scarce, it was a way to play a game with your own mind—to feel more reconciled to your lot than you would be otherwise. Actually, now that I think

3

about it, both our parents often stressed the importance of always eating *mit Verstand*—"with understanding," with an awareness of the preciousness of food, with gratitude and thankfulness

Acute myocardial infarction

It was a morning in June in 1990, and I was stuck in a pocket of empty time in my second-floor apartment in southeast Fresno. Gentle morning sunlight flowed inside between the Venetian blinds on the living room window. My suitcase and carry-on luggage stood at the ready close to the front door, already fitted out with the requisite identification tags. It must have been around nine o'clock or so; I was reviewing my travel plans, double checking my flight itinerary and passport and cash reserves, and getting ready to call a cab to take me to the airport.

I was all set to fly to Frankfurt am Main and then go by train to Halle, a city located in the former East. The university there was hosting a conference about the recent fall of the Berlin Wall and the imminent unification of the two Germanys. As a German teacher at Edison High and as the son of German immigrants, I was eager to learn as much as possible about this pending event and to gather materials that I could use in my classes. The conference was geared toward high school instructors like me as well as others at the college and university level.

The fact that the conference was slated to take place in Halle was not without its appeal. At that time in the Nineties I still knew relatively little about my father's past—especially his life before he came to the United States. Only on a few isolated occasions had he told me that he'd spent several months in a slave labor camp in Wolmirsleben, a village close to Halle. It seemed feasible that, in the course of my stay there, I might be able to glean more information about those turbulent times in general and Wolmirsleben in particular. Overall, the reunification of Germany opened up the opportunity to travel more easily in the former East and, by extension, the chance for me to learn a whole lot more about my family history.

My phone rang; it was my mother calling from Lodi. At first she sounded like her usual self—but then she didn't sound that way at all. Her words became increasingly scattered and unfocussed, something that just wasn't like her. I remember her telling me—at great, excruciating length—about the flowers in her garden, about how lovely they looked. Finally, after several minutes or so of a virtual monologue, she let me know why she was calling— my father had passed away during the night.

It had been his third heart attack; he'd been lying on the tan couch in the living room when it happened. My older sister Ursula had been the first to notice that something was amiss with him. He was rushed to the emergency room at Lodi Memorial Hospital, where he was pronounced dead later that evening, at 11:30 PM. His death certificate showed acute myocardial infarction as the immediate cause of death.

He'd celebrated his sixty-third birthday a few months earlier, in April.

And so the shape and feel of my morning shifted completely. I made a long-distance call to Arizona and left a message for the professor who'd arranged for me to attend the Halle conference; then I contacted my travel agent and let her know I'd be cancelling my flight. I talked with the next-door neighbors, the ones who'd promised to collect my mail and take care of my cat Tribble. Inside a few moments the day had morphed into a wholly different sort of day, one with a different and solemn rhythm.

Mosaic of images

My mother passed away several years later, on February 22, 2014, after a lengthy and grueling bout with Alzheimer's. Ursula had cared for her in our old family home in Lodi, and the strain of that responsibility had clearly taken its toll on her. I'd driven up to Lodi several times each month to help out, mostly on weekends, running errands to the pharmacy and buying groceries for both of them. During that period we hired an array of part-time caretakers, but the lion's share of taking care of Lisa, as we now called her, fell on Ursula, and she was plainly devastated when our mother passed away early that day.

I was down in Fresno that morning, cooling my heels at a muffler place along Blackstone Avenue, waiting for my Acura to be repaired and using my time to mark a stack of AP English essays. When I got back to my house, it was already close to noon, and when I saw that Ursula had left a voice mail for me, I got in touch with her. She was crushed, deeply shaken—and, unfortunately, as had become her habit, using alcohol as a crutch to deal with the strain and trauma of that moment.

In the next few days my brother Tom flew out from his home in South Carolina to help with the arrangements for cremation. Although we tried to contact our sister Barbara during those days, leaving a slew of messages on her voice mail, she kept her distance from us. That wasn't surprising; she'd grown estranged from the rest of us for quite a while, in part because of the shock she felt after our mother began showing symptoms of Alzheimer's.

During the three days that Ursula, Tom, and I spent together in the old family house things were a little cramped. I wound up sacking out in the master bedroom, lying on what had, for years, been my father's side of the bed. Facing me on the eastern wall was an array of small framed color photographs that my parents had assembled over the decades, documents of their life together. Before I drifted into sleep on those evenings I found myself studying that mosaic of images. One of them was a Christmas portrait snapped in the living room and probably hailing from the early Seventies.

Another showed us children sitting in the backyard, in our 1963 incarnations.

Most of them, though, just featured our parents standing together, mostly in Yosemite or some other nature location.

Looking at this display led me to recognize how little I actually knew of their lives together—their lives as individuals and as a couple, beyond their familiar roles as father and mother for the four of us. We'd known and related to them as our parents, but their past was for the most part hidden behind a closed door of virtual reticence.

So who was this woman who had just passed? And who, in reality, had her husband been?

What could I really see and understand in this wall of memories, and what sorts of things would I never be able to fathom?

"Jeepers Creepers"

When I grew up in Lodi in the Fifties and Sixties, my parents' German heritage was very much a part of my life and my siblings' lives. For starters, the default language in the home was always German; English was reserved for times when guests came by to visit. A framed black-and-white photograph in the living room showed a stern, knowing face of Therese Reiner—our aunt, or so our parents claimed back then.

My brother and I often played with a succession of wooden Matador sets which hailed from *Deutschland*, each of them replete with a booklet of illustrations showing an array of contraptions that could be constructed, the gizmos growing progressively more intricate and sophisticated with each set we acquired.

Our cuisine at home was typically Germanic, due in part to an old-world butcher in Sacramento whose store my father regularly frequented. Our grandmother often prepared lumpy but tasty mashed potatoes, and each December our mother baked a tasty fruit cake called *Stollen* and a wide-ranging assortment of German Christmas cookies. One of my fondest childhood memories involves helping her to prepare platters with an array of these holiday *Plätzchen* and then going around the neighborhood with my father to knock on acquaintances' doors and deliver these holiday gifts.

The first language that I heard and imbibed was German— or, actually, a German heavily flavored with a Bavarian dialect, especially in my father's case. My parents had both taken pains to learn English, but despite their best efforts their pronunciation usually betrayed their immigrant roots. My mother, for her part, had first learned Oxford English, which was often a far cry from the lingo typically spoken in the California's Central Valley. Once, at our regular grocery store, she asked a clerk where she could find Neopolitan ice cream, something that I could understand easily enough, but it was a set of sounds that perplexed the clerk to no end. My father's English hailed only partly from formal classroom instruction. He'd apparently also picked up a string of English idioms and phrases during his time in the U.S. Army as well as during his years working at Super Mold, a tire retreading firm in Lodi— and a good number of those idioms were hopelessly old-fashioned. To pick one example: many times, when a particularly unusual or unsettling report appeared on the evening TV news, he would react by muttering "Jeepers Creepers"—something that no one but our dad ever seemed to say.

Inside our homes, however—first in the corner house at 1400 W. Locust Street and, later on, in the early Sixties, in a larger bungalow at 1223 Midvale Road in the spanking new Willow Glen development—they spoke in their native tongue, and we four children followed suit. My facility with English came over time, but it developed slowly, and that had consequences. Once, during my kindergarten year at Reese Elementary, I walked along the street to school and, within minutes of entering the classroom, began getting pinched by other kindergartners. I honestly had no idea why they were acting this way, and the torment seemed to go on and on. It turned out that it was St. Patrick's Day, meaning that everyone was supposed to wear something green to school, and those without green bore the consequences of that sartorial omission. Two of my classmates, though—Judy Wudel and Craig Yarborough—cut out a piece of green paper for me and, with our teacher's help, pinned it to my shirt, saving me from further misery and embarrassment.

Another time, also long before I'd developed a basic proficiency with English, I had to spend a few days and nights in Lodi Memorial

Hospital. My parents later told me that while I overnighted there I cried at night, asking nurses in German to bring me my *Heiedecke*. It was my good luck that one of the physicians passing by my hospital room—Dr. Ingeburg Kultzen—was fluent in German, and she promptly understood that I was asking for the soft, comforting blanket that I'd always slept with in my room at home.

Nor were those the only German touches that marked those early years. When our family went up into to Sierra Nevadas on vacation every summer, often renting a cabin at Strawberry, my father would take us on hikes or fishing expeditions along the middle fork of the Stanislaus River, and at some point—typically when he'd found an appropriate lookout point with an impressive view—he'd begin to yodel. It was clear that he'd only let loose with boisterous yodeling after he deemed the scenery to be worthy of his efforts, and it was something that definitely gave him a lot of boyish pleasure. For us children it was a foreign, exotic sound—something that, just like "Jeepers Creepers," we only heard from our dad and no one else.

Every year our parents also took us to at least one performance at the War Memorial Opera House in San Francisco—either *The Nutcracker* or, increasingly later on, operas like *La Traviata* or *Die Meistersinger* or *Aida*. My mother took care to check out the LPs of each year's opera from the Lodi Public Library well in advance of our trip to the big city. She told us about each opera's plot, and she played its main arias and choruses for us. That way we were primed for the actual performance; years before the introduction of supertitles we could all follow along with relative ease, having soaked up background details about each work's characters and themes in advance. Needless to say, the New York Met opera broadcasts often supplied the soundtrack of our Saturday mornings, including the opera quiz during one of the intermissions, something that our mother often excelled at. This too, smacked of the exotic and the unusual; it was grounded in a passion for concert music that our parents shared and cultivated, something that inspired and sustained them, and a passion that they were keen to share with us.

And yet, though the German language and fragments of German culture and customs were very much a part of our childhood, many key elements of our parents' past stayed very much in the shadows, obscure and opaque. They rarely shared much about their own youth in Germany, about the years before they came to the United States—except for occasional stories about Marko, a dog my mother had known years ago and whose memory she cherished. Beyond anecdotes about that dog, I don't remember them telling us much of anything about their own childhoods, about their own time at school, their home life, or vacations that they took when they were young. Our father had clearly learned quite a bit about carpentry earlier in life. He had a workshop out in the garage that included a hefty concrete-gray toolbox stocked with all sorts of hammers, screwdrivers, and other sundry tools, and he often made things for use in our house—for example, a rectangular table top that we could carry into the dining room before guests arrived and secure on top of the regular, significantly smaller table and screw into place so that pretty much everyone—up to a group of ten—would be able to dine together. Our mother had obviously learned her sewing skills earlier in life. Many times in the afternoons and evenings she busied herself at her Singer machine next to the service porch, and she must have picked up that talent during her time in Munich as well. She also did prodigious amounts of knitting—for example, when we were watching television, she'd often sit in the back of the living room with knitting needles in her hands. Besides sweaters, she always made *Hausschuhe* for us—slippers that we always had to wear when we were inside the house, slippers that needed to be replaced with larger ones as we kept growing. These also functioned well as weapons of sorts; Ursula, Barbara, Thomas and I often lobbed them at each other in the living room and elsewhere in mock epic battles.

The Christmas season continued to be graced by presents from our German relatives—and if the Matador sets no longer came our way, then we could always depend on the arrival of a *Baumkuchen* from Munich—a "tree cake" rich in marzipan which was usually wrapped in a tasty chocolate coating.

Theresienstadt

Only by chance did I find out more about my grandmother's earlier life, thanks to a novel that I came across during one of my weekly library visits.

I must have been a seventh- or eighth-grader when I spotted a paperback copy of Leon Uris' *Exodus* and paged through it voraciously. Back then the Lodi Public Library on Pine Street was divided into two distinct sections, one for children and the larger one for adults, and most likely I'd once again disobeyed the formal rules by checking out the Uris book from the adult section, even though I wasn't officially supposed to do that yet. My father and mother both noticed that I was reading it and that its contents absorbed me—the people caught up in the Holocaust and being sent to camps, people fleeing to foreign countries later on, the rugged life in the early years of Israel, and the triumph of Israel becoming a new nation. Once evening after dinner, and after my siblings had left the room, my father spoke to me about it—not about its specific contents, though, but instead about his own mother—my Oma. I remember him standing next to the dining room table and facing me, meeting my eyes with a solemn expression that was unusual for him. Because I was reading that paperback, he felt that it was time for me to hear that my grandmother had been sent to Theresienstadt, a concentration camp located in Czechoslovakia, during World War II. He didn't elaborate on this very much, and at that moment I didn't have many questions for him. Our talk ended as abruptly as it had started.

Our lives in Lodi continued, and still my parents seldom spoke about their past. I remember my grandmother as always being reticent and somewhat withdrawn; it never occurred to me to approach her and talk to her directly about what my father had said, even though my curiosity had been piqued. We visited with her regularly every Sunday after going to mass at St. Anne's, and she usually joined us for dinner every Sunday evening. Despite all of those opportunities I don't recall ever approaching her with questions about her past. I probably felt that there would be no point to such questioning, that she'd decline to answer any questions about her past in general or her experiences in Theresienstadt in particular.

Once, when we were vacationing for a week in a rented cabin up in Strawberry, my older sister Ursula sat with Oma out on the deck, which overlooked a placid, picturesque meadow and the South Fork of the Stanislaus River. Oma was paging through a current copy of *Stern* magazine, something which one of our Munich relatives had sent over, when she suddenly froze and looked deeply afraid. Liselotte noticed that something was wrong and came out to find out what had happened. Apparently the magazine contained a lengthy article about the Holocaust that included information about Theresienstadt, the camp that our Oma was all too familiar with. One photo showed a door—and Oma explained in hushed tones what that door was and what lay behind it. Another time in the late 1960s, when I became enamored with an offbeat television show called *The Prisoner* and starring Patrick McGoohan, I shared my fascination about the series with her. She just looked grimly at me, nodded, and let me know that "I know what it's like to be a prisoner." It wasn't the sort of moment that invited more questions.

Then, around that time, our mother did share one anecdote with us. When she was growing up, her father, Karl Peschel, had helped to smuggle persecuted individuals—Jews and gypsies, among others—out of Nazi Germany. From time to time there were guests in the house, people who just stayed for a few days and then vanished. One of them, a gypsy woman, once read her palm and told her that she'd spend much of her life away from Germany, in another country far away. The story plainly resonated with her later on when the woman's words became true.

Wolmirsleben

In the succeeding years my parents told me a few more things about their past, but those moments were rare.

Back in the late summer of 1975 I was getting ready to fly over to Germany and study for a year at the Albert Ludwig University in Freiburg im Breisgau. The evening before my flight my suitcase and carry-on were packed and standing idly in a corner of the bedroom that I shared with Tom. After dinner my father asked me if I'd like to take a walk with him—something that we'd done fairly regularly ever since I'd been in grade school. Dusk was already gathering as we got going, and we headed west through the Willow Glen suburb and out to the placid waters of Lodi Lake. There, along its eastern shore, he found a picnic table and motioned for me to sit down. By that time the light had faded; the sun had dipped behind the trees, and the lights of the General Mills plant shone in the distance. The dark waves lapped rhythmically along the shore close to us, and all I could see across from me was his silhouette. Later on I came to suspect that he'd done that on purpose—that he hadn't wanted me to see his eyes, or maybe to look directly at mine, during the conversation that we were going to have.

He reminded me about *Exodus*, which I'd read a few years before, and about the brief talk we'd had about it once after dinner. Now that I was set to go to Germany—and, among things, to meet some of our relatives in Munich—he wanted to fill me in on some further family history. Abruptly, without much embellishment, he told me that he'd been sent to a labor camp himself. Beyond sharing that fact he didn't pass on many particulars about the site—not even its name, nor how long he'd been held there. Years later I found out that the place was called Wolmirsleben, and that he'd been held there for several months.

Another isolated glimpse into his past happened in the early Eighties when he took a business trip to the Eastern United States for his company, Aerojet General, and found some time to visit me in Toronto, where I was doing graduate work in Comparative Literature. When he came to Massey College, the Oxford style graduate student dorm where I lived, I treated him to a few sherries at the Common Room bar. After some tasty rounds and small talk he told me how he'd wound up reuniting with my mother after he and Oma had emigrated to the States. It turned out that he'd entered the U.S. Army in the early Fifties and completed his basic training at Fort Ord, close to the Pacific Coast. One day—he was slated to ship out to Korea on the very next morning—he and other privates were out on a training maneuver. A jeep pulled up, and its driver called out for "Private Roesch." My father was hustled back to the base and promptly given a German test. Needless to say, he passed it easily, and given his language skills his destination changed. Now, instead of Korea, he'd be going to Berlin to work in Army intelligence.

When I retired from my teaching job in the summer of 2016, I found the time to start translating the letters, postcards, and assorted documents that my brother and I had discovered in the family house after our older sister Ursula had passed away. My translation work gradually developed into a regular and fruitful routine. Early in the morning, after playing through some Bach two-part inventions and the like on the piano, I'd make a second cup of coffee, turn on the computer, begin streaming the classical music on Capital Public Radio, and launch into two or three hours of concentrated translating. The choice of the Sacramento radio station was hardly random: it was the station that our mother and Ursula often kept on during the day for many years in Lodi, and it was the one that Ursula and I tuned into for several hours a day when Liselotte succumbed to Alzheimer's and we were caring for her in the old family home in Willow Glen. Somehow it seemed more than a little appropriate to let this station provide the backdrop for my efforts. It had accompanied Ursula and me and bolstered our spirits as we took care of our mother during the final phase of her life. More generally, it reminded us of the gift of music that our parents had shared with us, and by extension everything else that they had given to us.

Ernst und Liselotte's correspondence spanned from 1945 to 1952, and it traced the development of their long-distance courtship and then their unlikely engagement and marriage. During much of this period Ernst was in Lodi, California, where he'd moved with his mother, Amalie. Liselotte Peschel, however, still lived and worked in Munich, making it highly improbable that they'd ever actually meet again face to face later on, much less marry and raise a family.

I wasn't injured at all...

The contents of the early letters made it clear that Ernst felt indebted to Liselotte because she'd stood by him and had his back in a time when, as a half-Jew with a Jewish mother, he lived at the margins of society and felt the dark weight of societal prejudice.

Liselotte not only sympathized with his plight, but also admired his scientific knowledge and his budding design and engineering abilities.

Although most of the correspondence was handwritten, some of the letters were typed, and many of them included unexpected decorations. Once Ernst had gotten into a ski accident in the High Sierras; in his next letter to Liselotte he included a splinter of his left ski. He taped it to the first page of the letter that he penned on May 15, 1948.

You might be wondering what that piece of wood is supposed to mean, and so I'll tell you about it right away. Yesterday I went skiing again at Sugar Bowl. There was a terrible snowstorm—the first substantial snowfall of the year—and this time luck was once again especially on my side. [in English] *I broke my skis.* [in German] *I wasn't injured at all, and fortunately I could get a single ski of the same type at the ski center. It comes from someone who'd also broken a ski, and that's how I luckily came to own a pair of skis again.*

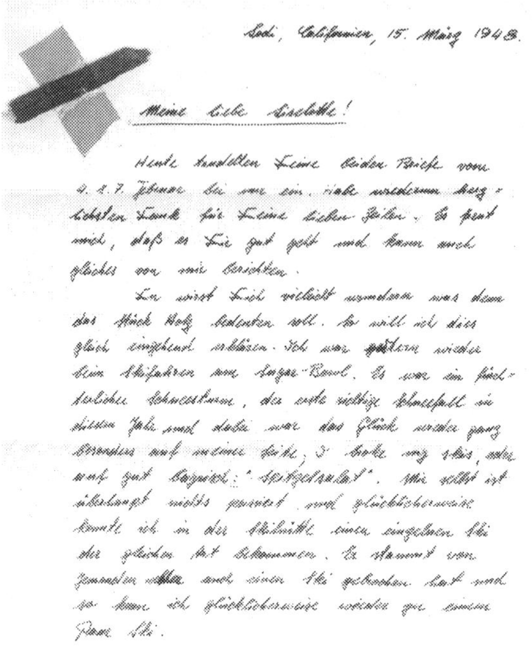
Lodi, Californien, 15. März 1948.

Meine liebe Liselotte!

Liselotte did similar things in many of her own letters. Once she spied a small flower peeking out of the snow close to her home, and she plucked it and attached it to the top of her next letter, dated October 5, 1947.

The flower comes from the garden; it's an autumn rose. I hope it can still be recognized when it gets to your house.

She enclosed something similar about a year later.

October 3, 1948

Here where we are there's a wonderful feeling of autumn, and I'm including some leaves from the trees in our garden. They have beautiful colors, and this way you'll also experience our autumn.

Do you also have something like this where you are?

I hope that you don't make fun of me when you see these leaves, but I really like them a lot. Once again I send you many greetings.

Your Liselotte

On yet another occasion she prepared her own Christmas card for my father and included it with a letter. She only had a few colored pencils at her disposal, though, which made the finished product look plain and childlike, even incomplete.

The letters and postcards had been organized according to their years of origin in brown expanding folders; my mother's handwriting indicated which year or years were contained in each one. The individual letters had been placed into clear plastic folders so that they were in mint condition when Tom and I came across them. Though the flowers, twigs, and leaves that Liselotte had often attached to many letters had faded—sometimes only a light green smudge remained on the spot where one of them had been secured—the content of all of the letters was accessible, and sometimes they were easy to read. There were exasperating exceptions to this rule, though. Ernst's spelling tended to miss the mark when he included English words and phrases, for example when he referred to a "ski tripe" instead of a "ski trip." When he went to the U.S. Army in the early Fifties, he began typing some of his letters, and his frequent typos made deciphering this part of the correspondence a particularly thorny challenge. Once my mother attended a carnival [*Fasching*] party in Munich that lasted pretty much the entire night, and immediately afterwards she wrote my father a lengthy letter on a lightweight sheet of airmail paper. Her handwriting was tiny as she tried to fit in as much as possible about the evening, even writing vertically along both margins, and the messiness of her penmanship suggested that she was still more than a little tipsy after that all-night bash.

To my dismay several of the letters had been censored. In some cases an eight-page letter—the pagination was indicated at the top of each sheet—had been reduced to about four, and certain sections of the remaining pages had been neatly cut away, sometimes in mid-sentence. I remember that in the early Seventies my parents' marriage had gone through a rough patch. My father had withdrawn now and then to gather and read some of the old correspondence, and then he'd show my mother what she'd written back then—something that tended to lead to a new round of altercations. I'm assuming that at some point our mother decided to take away some of those sections so that he couldn't use them as ammunition against her any longer. Another possibility, of course, is that later on, maybe after Ernst passed away, she went through the letters and removed and destroyed portions that she wanted no one else, not even any of us, to know about. Whether or not that's true, I know for sure that after my father passed away in 1990 she found a detailed journal that he'd meticulously kept for several decades. After paging through some of it, she decided to burn it, telling me later on that since he'd opted to keep his journal private, it was something that he hadn't wanted us to have access to. I still have a problem accepting her decision to do what she did and forgiving her for it. I also wonder whether she actually destroyed that journal so as to honor our father's privacy. It could well be that some of those pages contained details of the darker moments in my parents' marriage, something that she didn't want us to ever be exposed to.

Let's hope that we can see each other again soon!

I organized the contents of each folder in chronological order and set to work rendering them in English, sometimes getting help from a few native speakers in town when certain words, phrases, or snatches of handwriting proved too devilish for me to unravel on my own. The first item—and the only one that stemmed from the year 1945—was a postcard that Ernst wrote on April 25th, when he was already imprisoned in Wolmirsleben. The peanut-brown card had a six-cent Adolf Hitler postage stamp printed in the upper right corner and, at the bottom left, an exhortation to readers to devote their lives to supporting Hitler in all of his efforts: *All that our leader knows is the struggle, work, and worry; we want to do all that we can to ease his burden.*

On the back side of the card my father wrote a short note, wishing her all the best for the Easter holiday:

Dear Miss Peschel!

I'm rushing to send you these very, very affectionate Easter greetings. Here where I am nothing at all has changed. Let's hope that we can see each other again soon!

Most affectionately,

Your Ernst

When he started writing to Liselotte, he addressed her using the formal *Sie*—not the more casual and familiar *du* that you'd reserve for family members, close friends, and significant others. Later on, without warning, he switched to the *du* address, something that caught Liselotte off guard and that she at first took exception to. Ernst clearly entertained and nurtured hopes that their correspondence would lead to something far closer, and he'd already developed powerful feelings for her, something that she often wrote about openly. Many times she warned him about this in her responses, reminding him that they now lived thousands of miles away from each other.

Then, almost as abruptly and unexpectedly as the way that my father had started writing to her with the familiar *du*, her tone shifted and she became more encouraging and affectionate. She also repeatedly assured him that, even though she sometimes went to social and cultural events with a certain man, that friendship was by no means romantic in nature. For example, in March 1948 she attended an opera with him, something that troubled Ernst when he read about it. In a later, undated letter from the same year she responded to the concerns that he'd raised.

Now, regarding what you wrote: once again, don't concern yourself or worry about my going to the theater, because I didn't even go there that often with that man, and I also don't intend to at all, because usually I always go to plays with Gisela and Miss Reiner, or with other acquaintances (but also with ladies or with married couples—nothing for you to be concerned about). It's just that this particular man has some connections so that he can get opera tickets, something that I couldn't ever get myself, and so I went twice to the opera with him and twice to the State Theater. But, dear Ernst, I'm asking you not to be worried about this. Once, a long time ago, I even wrote to you that I know several men. That's obvious, of course—from school, from work—but you know very well that a person can just converse with someone and, after all, you know what my position is. And so I hope that I've explained that to you well enough, and that you understand my words correctly—what I hope and believe, and that I'm asking you not to be upset about this. Consider that I even wrote to you about this, that I'd gone out with this man, and so it's clear that I'm not harboring any secrets from you—and that speaks a lot in your favor, don't you think? So, dear Ernst, I'm asking you once again to understand all of this the right way—all right? Otherwise I'm sorry that I wrote to you about it, if you're getting upset about it now.

As I worked my way through the folders, this change of heart puzzled and intrigued me. Why had Liselotte decided to encourage his hopes? What she'd written to him at first was plainly true: they were now leading lives in very different parts of the world, and the odds that they'd see each other again, much less that he'd have the opportunity to court her, were slim at best. I assumed that part of the answer had to do with the harsh conditions in Munich in the postwar years, circumstances that didn't seem to improve as the Forties ended and the Fifties began. In one letter, dated March 17, 1947, my mother wrote about her evening English classes.

Just imagine: last Saturday, on the 15th of March, it snowed again here. You know, even though snow is beautiful, we'd be quite satisfied if we got no more snow for the rest of the winter. In Munich we've had cold ranging from 25 to 27 degrees; I was freezing quite a bit at work, but pretty much everyone else has had to endure this. Most of all we were freezing after work when I went to language school, because there we were sitting for one-and-a-half hours in an unheated room. Some of the windows had no glass in them; instead they were covered with cardboard.

There we could really have used some of the heat you have in California. Now, though, it's gradually getting better for us. We're all very happy about this, and we're looking forward to the warmer time of year.

In early October 1948 she also wrote about the dangers that she sometimes had to contend with.

Now it's already getting dark here at this time. You can feel autumn in the air, and above all you feel how short the day is. For me this time of day is always a little discomforting because of the time that I walk home from my evening classes. However, when it comes to assaults—and unfortunately we've had quite a lot of those incidents—the situation has improved substantially. One time two Poles followed me; don't even ask how I was able to get back home. I was dripping with sweat because I'd been running so fast, and I was white as a wall. They were always saying such crazy things in broken German. But that was back in the winter of 1946. So, all in all, I'm not really afraid about such things now.

Some basic utilities were also lacking during this period, as she shared on October 5, 1947.

In the evening hours during the week (eight to nine-thirty) we don't have any light; that's really very terrible.

Rising prices also caused her grief.

January 28, 1950

I'll start my new job on Wednesday. In my next letter I'll you all about what I think about it. It's really ideal that I can walk there and that I don't have to spend money for the streetcar fare. One single fare now costs twenty-five cents here! That's insane!

Unfortunately I can't send you my picture today along with this letter...

For his part, my father firmly believed that this was the woman he was fated to marry, and he never appeared to waver from his deep-seated conviction. Soon he began to end his letters with a signature phrase—*Your Ernst, Who is Always Faithful to You*—or some permutation of this sentiment. At one point he asked her to send him a photograph of her. She replied to his request on October 5, 1947.

Last Friday I got your letter of September 23, 1947. Thanks so much! Once again it hadn't been opened, which is why it came here so quickly. Unfortunately I can't send you my picture today along with this letter, because it takes a long time here for photos to be developed. Also, I can't send you any "pictures," but just a single one; I don't really get that many because the paper is in such short supply.

Although he had to wait several months, she finally did send a picture to him, a black-and-white photo that he kept next to his bed in his room in the Lodi apartment.

So what led to this change? I was even more baffled because one of the brown folders held numerous letters written to my mother by Hermann John, someone she'd often seen and dated in Munich during the late Forties—clearly, the man she'd gone to the opera with. The photo albums that my mother had sedulously assembled contained numerous pictures of road trips that the two of them had taken—to the Triberger Waterfall in the Black Forest, for example, among many other scenic places.

Liselotte's correspondence with Hermann John went on even after she married Ernst in 1952. At that time Hermann wrote her fairly lengthy letters that focused on his job at Siemens, including a period that he spent working in India for several months. He made sure to send her a card congratulating her on the occasion of her wedding. In the years that followed he wrote candidly to her about his private life and dreams. He let her know about the vicissitudes and tribulations he faced in his quest to find a wife for himself—the notices that he placed in the personal section of the newspaper, for example—and later, in July 1955, he sent her the announcement of his engagement to Ursula Zeutzschel. He also made sure to send her the formal announcement of their wedding, which took place in late November 1955 in Düsseldorf-Oberkassel, something that Liselotte likewise took care to preserve. Their friendship clearly meant a lot to her, given the time and care she'd devoted to organizing not only the relevant pictures but also Hermann John's letters alongside my father's. So, given that this relationship was so special and important to her, why had she opted to marry Ernst?

Before I flew to Europe in the fall of 1975 to study in Freiburg, my mother made sure that I had Hermann John's address in Munich. She wanted me to meet him personally; it was important to her that this would happen, and during Christmas break I took a train trip to Munich and spent an enjoyable afternoon with him at his home. He impressed me as being a highly intelligent, self-possessed man—civil and watchful, observant and well spoken. Although his wife had passed away recently—my mother had told me about her sudden and tragic death—he betrayed no sense of mourning or melancholy during our time together. Neither did he speak very much about my mother, other than asking how she was faring in California.

So, I found myself wondering, what had transpired so that, in her later letters, my mother did an about-face and nurtured my father's hopes? What had happened that made my parents' courtship and eventual marriage and real possibility and then a reality?

CHAPTER TWO

Stars

The marriage is up to fifty-three percent positive.

*O*nly later on, as I made my way through my parents' records, did I come across a detailed eight-page document that shed some light on this puzzle. It was an astrological report entitled *Character Description, Outlook for the Future, Comparative Analysis,* and it had been prepared by Eduard Bachmaier—a "Private Scholar" in Munich, as the return address on the back of the envelope boasted. There's no indication about when Herr Bachmaier was given this assignment, nor when he completed it.

Herr Bachmaier began with Liselotte Peschel, noting that she'd been born on January 14, 1927, at 8:45 Middle European Time in Munich, and proceeding to analyze her personal traits and those of her ideal mate. Based on her astrological chart, he felt that Liselotte had diverse interests, an ability to nurture harmony, and a need for change and diversion. Taken together, these precipitated fluctuations in her moods and feelings, making it imperative that she select a marriage partner with a calmer disposition. Choosing the best partner would be challenging in her case, though, *because various relationships are being maintained and it's hard to decide which man is your true love.* To remain faithful she'd need to cultivate a close relationship with her partner. Should that fail to happen, she could easily be tempted to maintain friendships in addition to the marriage, something that could easily sabotage it. *An abundant exchange of views and ever new intellectual challenges will be necessary for you and your partner to stay attracted to each other.*

Some of this does in fact sound a lot like our mother. She definitely initiated and maintained a large number of long-term friendships during her life, and she did indeed have a lively personality that radiated exuberance and a strong love of life. She was particularly adept at forging long-lasting friendships during her travels in Europe and elsewhere. In her later years, before her health problems overwhelmed her, she maintained an active correspondence with many of these people in several corners of the globe.

Compared to the astrological portraits of Ernst and Hermann that follow, Liselotte's is only page long, and it doesn't include a heading, making it likely that what's left in the file is the second page of a description that originally ran for three or more pages. Someone— most likely our mother herself—removed these other pages. Several letters in the other folders, as I've already mentioned, showed signs of having been heavily censored.

The astrologer then spent two pages considering the case of Hermann John. He sensed that Herr John was far more emotional than others might think, and he detected a lively intellect as well as an ongoing need for support from others. All in all, John's was *a pleasant personality* with *a strong need for love.* He was *genuinely searching for love without always recognizing that authentic love also requires a strong and constant reciprocal love.* He harbored a staunch sense of family and a rich emotional life, and he valued a harmonious organization of domestic life. He had a sober view of things and a practical sense of life that included a propensity to make money. His chances for a successful career weren't at all bad, with the exception of some periodic setbacks. With regard to marriage he might, at first, hesitate to make a commitment. Outside of minor tensions, Herr Bachmaier concluded, a marriage with Liselotte should be a harmonious one.

He rated Herr John's horoscope as being 46% positive.

Next he offered a portrait of Ernst Roesch, born in Munich on April 15, 1927, at eight o'clock. In Ernst he perceived great sincerity, high moral standards, and a tendency to view things intellectually. Ernst found *lots of pleasure in reading and studying,* and he was adept at *sharing his ideas, both orally and in writing.* Overall, he was someone who took life lightly. When it came to matters of the heart, he had a strong need for love and would, to some extent, come to depend on his partner. A reliable person with a deep-seated sense of justice, he also yearned to be recognized and valued. He was interested in sports, desired harmonious relationships, and cultivated an aesthetic sense as well as an artistic sensibility. As with Liselotte, he enjoyed *a rich inner life* and had *a wide spectrum of interests.* The astrologer foresaw many difficulties entering Ernst's life in terms of his health and other life-threatening dangers that would have to be confronted. Altogether, though, Ernst had a successful life in front of him, *both in his career and in his private affairs.* He would *live to an age well beyond that of the average person.* His sober, practical view of life would help him to overcome adversity.

In his conclusion Herr Bachmaier rated the horoscope as being positive *up to fifty percent.*

It's interesting that Ernst's character description goes on for three full pages, whereas Herr John's description lasts only two. Hermann John's section is definitely complete as it appears here, as Ernst's also seems to be.

Although some of this paints a somewhat accurate portrait of the man I knew as my father, some key details fail to hit the mark. My father never had much of an interest in sports, for example, and he died suddenly when he was only sixty-three. Beyond that, it would be far from accurate to claim that he took life lightly. For him, life was a profoundly serious business. I remember sometimes thinking as a boy that "Ernst"—as in "earnest"—was an especially apt name for him.

How might things look if Liselotte Peschel were to marry Hermann John? Herr Bachmaier weighed their prospects in some detail in the *Comparative Analysis* that followed.

His assessment of this possible match makes for fairly dismal reading. Liselotte and Hermann would rein in each other's development, and their attraction to one another would be short-lived. *One thinks, of course, about being happy together, but it's more a case of an infatuation that leads to aversion.* He could only locate a few positive factors in such a bond; it was focused on physical love but would give rise, with time, to *an unharmonious sexual relationship.* Various influences would lead to upsetting events and even cause great suffering for them both.

He rated the marriage prospects as being forty-five percent positive—though, given his gloomy comments, they would seem to merit a much lower percentage.

By contrast, a match between my mother and Ernst Roesch had a much rosier outlook, as the following section professed.

Ernst's and Liselotte's personalities complemented each other, Herr Bachmaier asserted. They were bound to each other intellectually and spiritually, and they felt a keen sense of duty for one another. Unlike a union with Hermann John, Liselotte's marriage with Ernst would exhibit lasting feelings of affection and an ongoing sense of reciprocal loyalty. It would be *a happy relationship that takes the form of a refined sensual love.* Both of them would tend to think loving thoughts about one another and would in fact be constantly united in their thoughts; they'd share happy, joyous experiences and also grapple with life's problems together. Even though they'd often be separated due to the demands of a career, they'd maintain their bond by writing letters to each other. Toward the end of his commentary Herr Bachmaier conceded that their life together might not always be blissful, acknowledging that *emotional turbulence isn't an impossibility*—something that could undermine their relationship *because of the oversensitivity or the weakness of one partner.*

Although the astrologer saw the marriage as being up to fifty-three percent positive, his remarks suggest that a much higher score was warranted.

He signed his report with a typewritten *B* and then added, almost as an afterthought: *The more favorable relationship is doubtless the one with Mr. Roesch.*

My mother's parents raised her as a Catholic, and she was thoroughly familiar with that faith's traditions and rituals. Still, somewhere along the line—I sense that her father played a profound role in this—she veered away from a strictly Catholic perspective. She shared this with Ernst in a letter written in Munich and dated April 22, 1951.

By the way, I don't regularly go to church, but I don't think that that's so bad. A person can also lead an upright life this way.

At this early time in her life I imagine that she'd already developed a powerful sense of a divine force in nature, and her pantheism guided her throughout the rest of her life. It was something we especially noticed whenever we hiked with her in the Sierras or strolled through our neighborhood in Lodi with Waldi, our longhaired dachshund, in tow. She also felt the sublime and the transcendental in music, especially in the universe of opera; and, perhaps because of her own mother, she also nourished a strong conviction about the value of astrology. She espoused a rock-solid belief that the stars do indeed guide and influence our lives and our destinies. One of her favorite operas, in fact, was Verdi's *La Forza del Destino (The Force of Destiny)*. Another Verdi work that she deeply admired was *Un ballo in maschera (The Masked Ball)*, in which Ulrica, the fortune-teller, correctly predicts the circumstances of Riccardo's death.

Once Dr. Ingeburg Kultzen—our family doctor, the same pediatrician who'd helped me to get a hold of my *Heiedecke* at the hospital years earlier—criticized the way that she was raising her children. Although I never found out what Dr. Kultzen had specifically told our mother, I remember how she defended herself. She dropped by her office, showed her a book about astrology—Linda Goodman's *Sun Signs*—and let her know that, as a Capricorn, she was compelled to raise her children in specific ways. To her mind the matter was as simple and straightforward as that.

Her convictions about astrology as well as fate certainly played a role in her decision to pursue a relationship with my father and also maintain a close friendship, primarily through letters, with Hermann John.

I was bombed out of my house on January 7, 1945...

Using my parents' correspondence as well as other material—letters, postcards from other relatives and family friends, and various incarnations of my father's resume—I was able to get a better sense their lives during the war as well as later on, in the postwar Forties and early Fifties. Various aspects of their lives came into clearer focus with the help of scores of documents and hundreds of black-and-white photographs that came my way, both from my parents' expanding folders and also material that I found in the safe deposit box that they'd maintained at Farmers and Merchants Bank in Lodi.

Although the result was far from complete, it was a great improvement over what my siblings and I had known about previously.

My father, Ernst Roesch, was the only child of Franz Xaver Joseph Roesch and Amalie Roesch. His birth certificate, dated April 19, 1927, shows that he was born in the Red Cross Hospital in Munich.

My grandfather was Catholic, as my father's baptism certificate attests. Amalie, though, was Jewish. Social pressure of the era was one factor that eventually precipitated their divorce, something that deeply troubled my father for the rest of his life.

At a certain point Amalie and her son moved to Straubing, a village lying northeast of Munich in the Bavarian countryside, but later on they returned to Munich.

Due to the worsening conditions for Jews and others deemed racially inferior Amalie and Ernst both applied for the right to emigrate to the United States in 1940. They received a form letter, written in bureaucratic German, from Hugh Teller, the American vice consul at the American consulate in Stuttgart, on February 27, 1940. In it they were advised that they'd gotten a *Quotennummer* for the next few months, and that they could, at their own risk, travel to the consulate and present documents to verify that they wouldn't be a financial burden to the U.S. should they be allowed to enter the country. Other details about their aspiration to emigrate aren't available anymore. Whatever they did—whether they did in fact go to the consulate in person to press their case, for example—isn't clear.

In 1941 Ernst began a toolmaker apprenticeship in the Friedrich Reiner Telephone Company in Munich, and his training lasted for a total of three-and-a-half years. After completing his apprenticeship in 1944, he kept working at the same company and, according to his 1968 resume, he was primarily concerned with "drafting and design of tooling for molding precision plastic parts, and detail drafting in connection with manufacture of telephones and other electro-mechanical apparatus."

Liselotte, for her part, was also born in Munich.

A later version of her birth certificate, dated November 10, 1951, shows her father to be Karl Peschel, and it identifies her mother as Aloisia Doesch, a servant in his household at Hindenburg Street 27. The document goes on to note that *the husband of the child's mother, Master Electrician Carl August Bartholomäus Peschel, gave the abovementioned child his family name—"Peschel"—on May 3, 1943.*

It was only decades later that my mother let me know about what her birth certificate was hinting at. It was long after midnight after a New Year's Eve celebration at her house in Lodi in the early 2000s. I was sitting with her at the dining room table when she abruptly told me that Karl Peschel hadn't actually been her biological father. Aloisia Doesch had worked in his house, and an Italian businessman got her pregnant. Karl, a widower who already had two children, married her and raised Liselotte as his own flesh and blood. Her letters and the photo albums reveal that Karl cared for her deeply; in fact, his daughter Käthe was sometimes jealous because he occasionally favored Liselotte over her. I remember how ashamed she still was when she let me know about the true circumstances of her birth. She wasn't sure about the name of the Italian businessman who had fathered her, but she told me that his surname was apparently the same as one of the giants in Wagner's Ring cycle—meaning that his name was either Fasolt or Fafner.

I tried to console her, to let her know that it didn't matter anymore, but she would have none of it.

Karl Peschel presided over his own company, and among other products his firm sold distinctive lamps.

The text in one of his magazine ads sings the praises of these lamps' *sophisticated lighting,* something *which turns a beautiful home into a cozy one.*

One of these lamps graced the living room in our childhood home in Lodi. It was always an exotic item for us children; none of our neighbors had anything like it.

Liselotte's lifelong fascination with all things scientific certainly stemmed from Karl Peschel's line of work.

When Ernst worked at the Reiner firm, he had at least two important acquaintances, Liselotte as well as another young woman called Lore-Lies. At a certain point the Gestapo summoned his mother Amalie to report to their headquarters; she was subsequently transported to Theresienstadt, a concentration camp located in Terezin, Czechoslovakia. Losing the company and support of his mother was a harsh blow for Ernst, making the sympathy and support that Liselotte and Lore-Lies showed him even more important.

Liselotte recalled an episode from this period in a letter she wrote to Ernst much later, on January 14th—her birthday—in 1950.

Ernst, what you remember about the way things were back then in Miss Reiner's house—all of it is exactly accurate the way that you describe them. I was bombed out of my house on January 7, 1945, and I only came for a brief time on January 14th. I still remember how Lore-Lies and you congratulated me. And it was exactly at noon on January 16, 1945—you also still recall this so well—we were all three of us downstairs in the Kassenschrank [probably a restaurant], and that was where you told us about all of the drawings, etc., and then you took your leave from us. I still recall all of this as well as if it had just happened yesterday. You've already written many times about things that happened in the past where I was amazed that you still knew about all of them.

You are hereby required to report to the Gestapo Regional Headquarters in Munich…

My father "took his leave" from the two of them at that time because the Gestapo had now sent him a summons similar to the one that Amalie had received.

The date, January 3, 1945, appeared in the top right corner. Addressed to *Mr. Roesch, Ernst, born on April 15, 1927,* it ordered him to report later on that same month.

You are hereby required to report to the Gestapo Regional Headquarters in Munich, Brienner Street 50 (in the courtyard) on January 17, 1945, no later than 15 o'clock so that you can be assigned to an urgent work detail.

The form letter went on to list what he had to bring along—including enough food for three days, sturdy work clothes and shoes, and one to two woolen blankets—and its final paragraph warned him that he'd face dire consequences should he not appear at the mandated time. An official stamp, complete with an eagle and a swastika, appeared at the very bottom.

After finding his way to Brienner Street, Ernst was taken to a labor camp called *Rothenförde*, but then later transferred to "*Sammellaber Wolmirsleben*," a site close to the town of Stassfurt. There the Nazis intended to set up an underground factory in abandoned salt mines that would produce components for V–2 rockets, and he labored there under harsh conditions for several months. Specifically, Ernst was assigned to work four hundred meters underground in Shaft Seven of the Grube Maria salt mine.

United States forces liberated the labor camp in the middle of April in 1945. A bilingual certificate dated May 11, 1945 bears witness to his time there; the stilted English version reads as follows:

The designer Ernst Roesch…was brought January 1945 from the camp Rothenförde to the camp of this place. He is a so-called jewish half-cast of the first degree and has been arrested in order of a regulation of the Reichsführer SS Reichssicherheits-Hauptamt Berlin—with the special action of the "Gestapo" against jews and people belonging to the jewish race. Being political prisoner he was forced to work as subordinate handicraftsman.

The camp of this place was liberated by the American Army on 11.4.45.

By order of the Military Government camps commander.

The camps commander provided an illegible signature at the bottom of both the German and English versions, and a further illegible signature attests to its veracity.

The story that my father told me many years later was that he'd held on to a gold watch during his months in Wolmirsleben. Later he could barter with the watch to get himself a bicycle, and he pedaled the whole way back to Munich—a distance of well over two hundred miles—in the hope of finding his mother again and salvaging something of his former life.

In January 1945 the Peschel house was destroyed during an Allied attack on Munich. Karl Peschel's household had to be split up, and Therese Reiner invited Liselotte to live with her at her home. A grateful Liselotte took her up on her offer.

Arriving in Munich after his ordeal in Wolmirsleben, Ernst needed a place to stay and people to help him find work, and he was inspired to track down Therese Reiner, a boss who'd treated him well in spite of the tenor of those times.

At that time you'd changed because of the time you'd spent in the labor camp...

When he came to Therese Reiner's home and knocked on the front door, Liselotte opened it up.

They both recalled this moment in their letters following the war, specifically in May and June of 1948. On April 17, 1948 Liselotte wrote:

It just occurred to me, Ernst—weren't you in Prinzen Street around this time in 1945? But now I think that that only happened later on—yes, I think that was in May and June! At that time you'd changed because of the time you'd spent in the labor camp, and because of the way you looked I almost didn't recognize the "earlier Roesch" anymore. Please don't be upset if I tell you that, but I noticed the change a lot. It's very clear that such a terrible experience would have a huge effect on someone...Dear Ernst—you do understand me the right way, and you're not angry with me—please don't be angry—but it really was that way.

Her words led him not just to recall that unanticipated reunion with her, but also the ways in which Wolmirsleben had shaped him. On May 17, 1948, he reflected on her words.

You write that when I returned from the camp I was completely different. Hopefully I didn't act too boorishly, especially when I was interacting with you. If that was the case, please forgive me. I really didn't notice anything like that myself. But, believe me, when I was taken away at that time I didn't believe that we'd see each other again. Even after a few days in the camp I was forced to see just how correct my hunches had been, and I changed my way of thinking completely—that is, I would have been ready to do the impossible before I would give up. When, out of the blue, the Americans marched into the camp, I was spared of this almost futile struggle. My determination prevailed, and thus it happened that one Sunday afternoon I returned to Munich and went to Miss Reiner before doing anything else. The first person I saw again—I haven't thought about it up until this moment—was Miss Peschel. I can still see very clearly the way that your eyes were glowing when you opened the door. (Please don't laugh because I'm speaking about your eyes, but I even took the liberty of doing this when I was still an apprentice working in the Reiner firm. Do you still remember?) If, at that time, the person standing in front of you didn't look like the "earlier Roesch," as you wrote, but rather more like a plinth, then I ask you once again to forgive my behavior. Please! Again I want to stress that I fully understand what you wrote, and that I'm not angry with you in any way, of course, as you thought I might be. But, in connection with what you wrote, something that an American once told me in a completely different context is really true: [in English] *"Prison changes a man."*

Shortly thereafter a notification was published stating that survivors of the Theresienstadt camp who hailed from Munich and the surrounding area would be brought back. Ernst went to the place where the transport trucks were scheduled to arrive, hoping against hope that he would find Amalie there. Even though only a handful of trucks appeared, his mother was in fact among the people who had survived.

Thanks to Therese Reiner's support, Ernst could resume work at the telephone company. In August 1945 he labored as a design engineer at the O & K Geissler firm, a tool and dye shop in Munich, a position he held until May 1946.

During that time he and Amalie took steps to emigrate to the United States. The United States Consulate General in Munich issued a *"Certificate of Identity in Lieu of Passport"* to Ernst on May 17, 1946. In it he declared his intention to emigrate to the United States, along with his *mother, Amalie (born as Rau) Roesch, born at Ermershausen Germany, on May 17, 1897—German citizen.* The certificate also specified that he had one distinguishing mark: *scar on right knee.*

Upon their arrival in the States they spent some time living with relatives in New York City, where Ernst found work as a manual laborer, but soon he heard about a job opening at Super Mold, a company in Lodi, California. Amalie's brother Willie, who was already in California at that time and had purchased some land in Galt, probably helped him find out about this opportunity. Amalie and Ernst traveled by train across the continent and found their way to Lodi. Soon they moved into an apartment along Oak Street.

My mother and I are really happy in our new home.

When Karl Peschel wanted to know about working conditions in California, Ernst quickly provided an answer in a letter that hailed from October 1948.

Now to answer your father's question: Well, on average an American worker is paid about one dollar per hour. What I personally earn works out to $1.45 per hour, and that comes to a net salary of about two hundred dollars. When I was an unskilled laborer in New York, I earned sixty-five cents per hour. The work week in the U.S.A. is forty hours long. Overtime is paid at a rate of "time and a half," and this also applies to white-collar workers.

Later on they moved to another apartment on South Central Avenue. On September 3, 1948, he told Liselotte more about new digs that he and Amalie had found for themselves.

It's very late now, but I still feel that I definitely have to write to you. I've neglected you somewhat because we moved, and I just hope that you'll accept that as an excuse. But, you know, every evening I was busy painting the apartment; after that we moved out of one place and moved here, and we arranged all of the furniture, etc. My mother and I are really happy in our new home. It's really beautiful, with three rooms, a kitchen, and a bathroom. Besides that, it's in a wonderful part of town, actually at the edge of town, and if it weren't for the palm trees then I could almost believe that I was living among villas in Grünwald [a municipality in the Munich district]. *Maybe you're wondering why I did all of the painting myself. But in America practically everyone does this. You can buy the paint, already prepared for you, and doing this yourself saves you a pile of money.*

He shared more specific information about their new place on September 15, 1948.

We've already gotten quite used to our new apartment. It's especially pleasant that the landlords are helpful, friendly, and charming, and that they even speak German. They're a widow and her two daughters, and both of the daughters are teachers. The husband just died a few months ago. All of them were born here in America, but they still call themselves German. Their ancestors emigrated from Württemberg to Russia around the year 1812, where they established German settlements in the area around Odessa…and so they were able to stay fluent in German. And so it was that cities were established in Russia with such names as Berlin, Kassel, etc.; but still, after a hundred years, they were required to become Russians. To avoid this many of them went to the United States and settled for the most part in the state of Dakota [not specified if this is North or South], *and there they've retained their German customs up to the present day. This is why the capital city of South Dakota is named Bismarck. However, many of these Schwabian immigrants decided to go to a part of the country that was more fertile, and our landlords belong to this group. They've already been in California for six years now, and they own a large vineyard here. They don't speak High German by any means, but rather, as they call it,* [in English] *low German.* [in German] *This, apparently, is something they inherited from their ancestors—an awful dialect with a tinge of Schwabian. But I'll let you know more about this another time.*

He described his daily commute to work on December 5, 1948.

I actually don't know if I've already told you that I'm one of the few bike riders in Lodi. I bought this when we moved into our new apartment because my workplace is now about three kilometers away. In any case riding my bike takes less time than the bus connection. You know, I don't have enough money yet to buy a car, and I don't want to buy an old one, because then you always have to get the car repaired and you're always broke. Quite honestly, I can't even drive a car yet.

Once, when I was passing through Lodi in 2017, I took the time to drive out to the small, modest house where my father and grandmother had once lived and then retraced the bike trip he must have taken up to the site of the former Super Mold plant. When I got there, I checked the odometer and transposed the full distance from miles into kilometers. As I should have known, my father's words were spot-on: the distance is exactly three kilometers.

A picture in one of the family albums shows him ensconced behind his desk at work:

Brief # 3   München, den 17. 3. 1947

Lieber Ernst!

Deinen Brief vom 1. März 47 habe ich bestens dankend
erhalten; er ist am 15.3.47 bei mir angekommen. Ich habe
schon oft gedacht, warum Du nie mehr etwas hören läßt,
denn Dein erster Brief kam ja schon im November vori-
gen Jahres. Hast Du eigentlich meinen Brief vom Dezember 46
auch erhalten, das war der Erste, und dann schrieb ich
den englischen. Wie lange brauchen die Briefe bis Du
Sie erhältst, ich denke schon 4-6 Wochen.

Stell Dir vor, bei uns hat es letzten Samstag, am 15.3., wieder geschneit; glaubst Du, ist schön der Schnee ist, aber für
diesen Winter würde es uns vollauf genügen. Wir haben
heuer in München 25 - 27 Grad Kälte gehabt; ich habe
im Geschäft auch ziemlich frieren müssen, aber so ging es
beinahe allen gleich. Vorallem abends, nachdem Geschäft,
wenn ich in die Sprachenschule ging, da haben wir erst
gefroren, denn 1½ Stunden saßen wir da in ungeheizten
Zimmer zum Teil ohne Glas, nur mit Pappe zu gemacht.
Da hätten wir eben etwas von Eurer Wärme haben sollen.
Aber, jetzt wird es auch bei uns allmählich wieder besser.
Wir alle sind recht froh und freuen uns auf diese Zeit.

CHAPTER THREE

Leisure

...I'll have to get up again at three o'clock.

$\mathcal{M}$y parents' correspondence became fairly regular once Ernst and Amalie settled in Lodi. What did they share with each other? Many of their letters actually dwelled on leisure activities, in particular time spent in the great outdoors.

My father was clearly enamored of the natural beauty that he found in California, especially in the High Sierras. Even though he'd explored parts of the Bavarian Alps earlier on, the likes of Donner Pass and Mt. Shasta opened up an entirely new and fascinating world for him. He didn't waste any time; he went skiing for the first time in California during December 1946, when he traveled up to Soda Spring.

He was fortunate enough to find a like-minded ski aficionado at Super Mold, Eddie Stritzel, and he often went on excursions to the Sierras with Eddie during his early years in the States. The mountain peaks in California overwhelmed and enraptured him, as the sheer amount of space he devoted to this topic in his letters bears ample witness to—not to mention the plethora of black-and-white photographs he snapped and then scrupulously organized in multiple photo albums. On April 12, 1947, for example, he wrote:

Now I'll have to wrap up this letter soon—first, because otherwise the letter will weigh too much; and second, because it's now 11:30 at night and I'll have to get up again at three o'clock. That's because some colleagues will pick me up at four o'clock to go skiing. We'll go by car into the California mountains, about 180 miles from here, and climb the mountain "Shugarball" [sp] *and "Sink-Belten"* [sp] *In my next letter I'll tell you all about it.*

What impresses me in passages like this is the sheer youthful joy and ebullience that he felt when he was there: many of the pictures show him looking straight into the camera and grinning heartily from ear to ear. Here was someone who, just a few years before, had faced more cruelty and inhumanity than I could ever conceive of, and now, just a short time later, he'd landed on his feet in the New World, working at a job that challenged his skills and creativity and relishing his sundry skiing and hiking trips.

Of course, he was quick to notice various differences between skiing customs in Germany and the United States, and he never hesitated to share his observations with Liselotte. Here, and increasingly in his later correspondence, he seasoned his German sentences with some occasionally misspelled English words and phrases.

April 27, 1947

The [in English] *"ski tripe"* [in German] *was really okay. Here there are lots of ski lifts and things like that, and so skiers really enjoy many conveniences. You know, of course, that Americans don't like to walk. I was surprised when I saw some skiers dressed in Lederhosen, traditional jackets and other related items of clothing. The strangest thing was this: the proud individuals who wore these clothes were mostly not even German, and even more rarely could any of them speak Bavarian German. Green hats and a chamois brush* [Gamsbart – used to decorate Alpine hats] *also aren't rare here at all, and those who count as true skiers here also know about our*

Edelweiss flowers. Some of them even try to yodel. When I brag that I was once in the [in English] *"Bavarian Alps,"* [in German] *then I always have to talk about our mountains. When I do this, my listeners are always amazed, and I'm always homesick. Up to now I always thought that it was impossible for me to speak very much about mountains. It's better if I don't tell you about the meals at all. They definitely weren't anything special. On the other hand, they prompted some memories, for example, the way you always used the bread stamps that you'd saved to treat me to dark gingerbead cakes. That definitely gave me more pleasure than all of the good and plentiful food that's here.*

His close friendship with Eddie Stritzel also made the challenges of living in a new country and communicating in a new tongue more bearable and surmountable.

At least one of their road trips took them to the Bay Area.

May 3, 1948

Now, you probably also want to know why I was in San Francisco. Well, I went there with my ski buddy; he needed to do some shopping there. I myself bought a sleeping bag there because we're planning to take a few extended skiing trips soon. Maybe I'll spend all of my vacation in the mountains; my friend and I actually want to climb up various mountains. I think that I've already told you about him. Actually, he's my only friend in the United States, and he works as a mechanic in my company. His wife is also a colleague of mine. Neither of them, of course, can speak German, but they really like me because I hail from the Alps, and I'm interested in the mountains and skiing. You should just hear the way he yodels. He can really do it very well. Just imagine—I've also learned how to yodel a little. I've told him about you. (I hope you don't mind.) He said right away that I should let you come over here; we definitely need someone who plays the accordion. Besides that, then all four of us could go to the mountains.

In a letter that probably stems from May 1948 he recounted an especially memorable and somewhat risky adventure that he undertook with the Stritzels. He seemed to list its dangers with a boyish pride, as if teasing my mother should she be in any way anxious or concerned about his safety.

Tomorrow I'm going to the mountains again to climb up Mount Shasta, the highest peak in California. Afterwards I'll tell you all about it, and I'll also send you photos.

In another letter, penned in late May of 1948, he went into greater detail.

Now I want to tell you about what's happening in my life. Just imagine this: I'll be going on vacation on the first of June, and actually this will be my first vacation in three years. My colleague, his wife, and I want go mountain climbing and skiing for the whole two weeks. We'll be going into the High Sierras, and so it won't even be that expensive; otherwise I wouldn't be able to do this at all. That's because in this area, in the High Sierras, there are neither cabins nor hotels. The region is just too large. We'll have to carry all of our food, etc. in our backpacks, and we'll spend the nights in a tent. I'm already very excited. Among other things we want to climb up to the top of Mount Shasta. This mountain is 14,300 [in English] *feet* [in German] *high, and it has three glaciers. Because of the long time it'll take to hike to the mountain and the difference in elevation we're figuring on two-and-a-half days' worth of climbing. In the mountains over here things are still a lot wilder than in the Alps. Bears are often in the lower elevations, and they really like to break into people's campsites. However, most of them are just looking for things to eat, like sugar, ham, or honey. In the higher elevations there might be wolves, wildcats, eagles, etc. Usually nothing bad occurs, but still many unfortunate things are known to have happened. My friend always brings along a revolver on his belt. I'm already looking forward to this a lot, and I'm happy that I have this opportunity. My mother, to be sure, is somewhat nervous, but when all is said and done she's given me her blessing to do this. Last year I took some* [in English] *"trips"* [in German] *like this a few times on weekends (Saturdays and Sundays). You know, it's really a fine thing to be sitting next to the campfire in the evening and cooking. It's something of an adventure, especially when you hear the howling of wild animals at night and you don't dare to get any sleep. Well, now I've told you about something unusual, haven't I? But please—don't be afraid. Nothing will happen to me. When I reach the peak of Mount Shasta, I'll write "Greetings from Bavaria" in German into the peak book. Of course, your positive thoughts will need to be with me, and I'll always carry along that small picture of you as a talisman.*

Now I have to tell you something else. I bought a hat, and I've decorated it with all sorts of things so that it now looks like a Bavarian mountain climber's hat. My skiing companions have done the same, and they're really proud [in English] of the Alpine-hat.

Sonora Pass played an important role in several letters of his, something that piqued my interest because, years later, he brought the whole family up to Sonora Pass on more than one occasion.

June 4, 1948

As I've already told you, I have vacation right now, and I'm using this time to accompany a co-worker and his wife on ski trips. The first week of vacation has already ended, and with that half of my vacation is gone. I was at Sonora Pass, and I climbed up various mountains, such as [names of mountains in English] Sevit Peak (11,575 feet high); Night Cap Peak (11,000 feet). [in English] We just cooked at the campfire, and we even spent the night out the open, underneath the sky, because here there aren't any huts, etc. You're completely cut off from the outside world. It was really quite beautiful, and we were even spared from any attacks by wild animals.

In another letter from June 1948 he shared much more about that trip, focusing on his time at Mt. Shasta.

I climbed up Mount Sevit (about 11,500 feet) and Night Cap (about 11,000 feet). You have to hike about five to seven miles to get to these mountains, something that's not that easy when you're carrying a large backpack. During the second week we went—always in the car, of course—to Mount Shasta City. We climbed up eight thousand feet to a cabin—owned by the Sierra Ski Club, which is similar to the Alpine Organization—and we stayed there for three-and-a-half days.

One snapshot that's survived shows Ernst standing in front of the Shasta Alpine Lodge, clearly enamored of his surroundings.

We were also completely alone up there, and we didn't even have to pay anything to be there. Then, without completing our goal, we left; the daily snowstorms had made it impossible for us to climb to the very peak of Mount Shasta (14,161 feet). The highest point that we could reach was 13,000 feet. If I'd just had an ice pick along with me, I wouldn't have given up in spite of the storm. On the way home we drove along the [in English] Redwood-Highway, [in German] *where the highest trees in the world can be seen (about one hundred meters high and with diameters of seven meters). All of this was very interesting for me, of course. In spite of all of this my thoughts were very, very much with you. I'll send you pictures of all of this so that you can get a sense of it. I hope that it's interesting for you, and I'll mail the pictures as soon as the films have been developed.*

On occasion, in the early 2000s, I got the chance to take some road trips up north to Redding and Lassen National Park, and sometimes much further north on I-V to places like Seattle. Mt. Shasta was particularly exhilarating—its majestic peak makes a dramatic and surreal appearance when you're heading north on the Interstate—and when my mother let me know about our father's experiences there, I got the idea that, maybe, at some point, Tom and I might climb up to its peak and complete the goal that he'd set for himself. A good friend of mine even bought me a hiking guide delineating the major routes that led to the peak. To date, though, nothing has come of this project.

On the other hand, many of the hikes that Tom and I have completed over the years were inspired by our father's earlier exploits and the hearty love of nature that he instilled in both of us.

His fascination with the Sierras never abated.

October 10, 1948

This Sunday afternoon will be devoted to writing an extra letter to you again. It's a wonderful autumn day, and if the weather continues like this, then I have a bad feeling about how the coming winter will be. My friend Stritzel is somewhat more optimistic, and whenever he sees me at work he talks about skiing. He even wants to start skiing in November to make the most of the skiing season. When it comes to the sport itself, that's fine with me, but I want to put off buying a new pair of ski pants for a while. Right now my mother is knitting a new pullover for me.

Ernst's skiing adventures provided him with relief and temporary escape from the occasional pressures of his job.

January 15, 1949

Today it's already very late, but still I don't want to neglect writing at least a small weekly letter. I hope that you're doing very well, and I especially hope that you're healthy. I'd have so much to tell you about, but I'll save it for another time. At the moment I'm always so very busy; you can't even imagine how much. But tomorrow I'll go skiing again; then my "interesting" work can go to hell.

For her part, Liselotte encouraged him to keep going on his sallies into the mountains.

March 2, 1947

Your story about the ski trip is very interesting, and I've already heard about Reno, Nevada—most of all I once read somewhere that a person can get married there really fast, and that you can also get divorced there in a hurry. I can imagine that there are lots of casinos there, and that you can probably lose more money than you win. But it's very good that you had the chance to go there; it's a change of pace for you. Even just traveling through the state and getting to know more about California is wonderful.

January 9, 1949

My dear Ernst! I hope that you've started out the new year on the right foot, and that you've already gone skiing, or that you'll soon go skiing, because otherwise you won't have any fun, no change of pace from your work. I hope that the snow conditions are better where you are, and I wish you lots of joy—but please, no broken skis. Here we've got skis made from aluminum, and they're supposed to be first-rate. There's no way that they can break. I personally can't ski, and I won't learn to do that anymore; I don't have any wish to learn that. Some people can do it so well.

At the close of this letter she added some local color.

During the night it snowed here. Today it looks wonderful; at least everything is white again. I always look forward to the snow. The small children who got skis at Christmas are already skiing along the street, or they're making their first attempts.

Three skiers struck it rich yesterday...

In some correspondence it also became apparent that Ernst was far from a mere dilettante when it came to skiing. He was especially proud of an event that he went to on January 16, 1949.

And so last I had a chance to do some serious skiing last Sunday. It was a great chance to relax. Just imagine—for the first time I entered a ski competition, and I even won a prize. It was the so-called [in English] *"49er Gold Rush Race."* [in German] *The other two winners were a former mountain ranger and a University of California student. The course was about one-and-a-half kilometers long, and I fell down along the way—but in spite of that I didn't lose much time. I really gave it everything I had...*

News of his prize was reported in a local newspaper; he preserved the complete article in his skiing album:

> Three skiers struck it rich yesterday in a 1949-style gold rush in the snow drifts. Lucky were Ernest Roesch, a mechanical engineer from Lodi, San Joaquin Country; Art Schimke, a veteran of the ski troops from Wilseyville, Calaveras County; and Robert Ramsey, a University of California student… Each staked a claim to one of three golden bags containing prizes, sponsored by the Amador Country Chamber of Commerce.

At some point, soon after he settled in Lodi, my father changed his name from "Ernst" to "Ernest," the American English equivalent. In his letters to Liselotte, though, he kept on using the German spelling for quite a while, probably because that was how she had come to know him and because they were, for the most part, writing to each other in German.

Ernst relished the chance to meet with other German speakers who shared his passion for winter sports.

January 30, 1949

I myself went skiing yesterday. It was just first-rate! I was in Squaw Valley, a new [in English] *ski-resort* [in German] *here in the Sierra Nevadas; it has the longest ski lift—it's two miles long. It was very cold, and when you're sitting for twenty minutes on a chair that's hanging from a cable so that you can reach the 9000* [in English] *foot Squaw Peak* [in German], *then you're really freezing. But the descent was fantastic. I went up on the lift twenty times to take advantage of the powdery snow, which is so rare here. I saw Emil Allais, who's a ski instructor there and who teaches his so-called "French method." You know, here there are skiers from every country that has mountains. And so I met a very nice Austrian man who's only been in the U.S. for seven months. It was completely by accident, and he was very reticent.*

But because the Austrians speak English in such a pleasant way—the same way that they speak German—I recognized his accent immediately. When I started to speak in German, he was very happy right away, and he wasn't embarrassed anymore about his English. But at first he didn't believe that I wasn't born in America. Only when I swore that I wasn't did he accept the fact that you can't learn this kind of German in the schools here. The cabin's very modern; I wish you would have been along. By the way, Eddie has a new car, and because of that the five-and-a-half-hour drive to get here was a lot more comfortable.

He also enjoyed the opportunity to observe other talented skiers in action.

March 17, 1950

Because I bought my car I've somewhat neglected going skiing, but tomorrow I'll take a trip and take advantage of the snow as long as it's there. I also went last week, more to see the race—the [in English] "National Giant Slalom," [in German], which was held at Mt. Lincoln—than to ski myself. Among the international participants there was the Austrian team, which included a female Olympic medalist. I spoke in German with many of them. In the meantime they're all back home in the Alps. Bavaria was also indirectly represented in the person of Lutz Aineder from Obersdorf, who's a ski instructor here. I saw him wearing a button that read "Ski Instructor" and began talking with him, assuming that he was Austrian. When he said that he came from Bavaria, I recognized the "White-Blue" of his button.

Bavaria's colors are white and blue.

He's only been in the United States for five months. He didn't do especially well in the competition. It's a good thing that he wasn't representing Bavaria in the race; instead he represented "Nebelhorn U.S.A." The Austrians, men as well as women, carried the day, and the United States came in at second place. But the Norwegians, Chileans, Swedes, French, etc. weren't bad. It's too bad that Bavaria didn't sent a team. Maybe they would have shown the Austrians a thing or two.

I also passed by the "L–E" tree again and I also took a picture of it.

During his time in the High Sierras Ernst found a tree that appealed to him—maybe like the yodeling locations that he found later on—and he carved Liselotte's initials and his own into its bark.

May 29, 1950

When I returned from my ski trip yesterday, your dear letter of May 21ˢᵗ was here to greet me. As always, of course, I was very pleased. The trip was very strenuous because of the heavy backpack that I took along, but we pushed ourselves until, at last, we were able to reach the top of Mt. Levit. It was cold when we spent the night up there at 10,500 feet, and the wind was raging around the tent. I also passed by the "L-E" tree again and I also took a picture of it. I hope that the picture will turn out well; if it does, then of course I'll send it to Munich.

Later on, during family trips to the Sierras, he took us up to see their special tree, and he gradually added all of our initials to the ones that were already there. A photograph in one of the early family albums shows Ursula and me standing proudly on either side of it, delighted to see our initials.

Beyond his road trips with the Stritzels, he also let Liselotte know about excursions to other places.

Sept. 15, 1948

Last Saturday our landladies invited us to drive to Sacramento with them because the state fair is happening there now. This is a mixture of a state exhibition and an Oktoberfest. I myself wasn't particularly interested in the flower exhibits, etc., because there was a so-called [in English] *Old German* [in German] *Biergarten there. Unfortunately, soon after we arrived the German band was replaced with a run-of-the-mill jazz band. This really disappointed me, but after I drank a few glasses of beer I also began enjoying this music. I just wrote "glass of beer," but actually the beer wasn't served that way by any means, but rather in paper cups. A Bavarian-style dance floor was also there, but instead of Schuhplattlern [a German dance] and waltzes people were dancing Buggi-Wuggi [Ernst's spelling] and other ridiculous sorts of things. The biggest similarity with a German outdoor pub was the presence of inebriated people.*

Sometimes, to Ernst's delight, people from his past life appeared unexpectedly.

June 4, 1950

As you know, of course, there was a holiday here on May 30th—meaning that there was no work—and I planned on being really lazy for once. Because of that I wasn't exactly thrilled when the telephone woke me up at 7:30. [in English] "Good morning, Ernest Roesch speaking," [in German] I shouted into the phone—and what came out of it was something that I couldn't make sense of: "Hello, this is Peter, Peter Hold, Professor of Engineering. Ernste, if this is the right number, if it's really you, then please just speak in German." Yes, this was really happening: it was a friend that I'd met back then in the labor camp. Now he was on a business trip in the United States, something that I'd actually known about because of our correspondence. So I was just as surprised as disappointed when I soon found out that he was calling from San Francisco and would be flying out at 12:30 that day. After we spoke for ten minutes I told him that I'd see him at eleven o'clock in the hotel, and soon afterwards I was sitting in my car, and I arrived on time in San Francisco. Can you imagine how it was? We were both, naturally, very happy. It's too bad that he couldn't come along back to Lodi, because the general manager was with him and every day of their trip had been arranged via reservations. But we had a nice conversation about all sorts of things, and after we talked I brought him and his boss to the airport. By the way, he'll never forget this car trip because San Francisco is really packed with traffic when you're going over all of these hills and then you drive out toward the airport. I drove quite moderately, but for him I was driving way too fast.

And so this brief reunion came to an end, and my friend will be at home again in Austria on the twenty-third, where he works at the Steyr-Daimler Puch Company and also as a professor at the university.

...I now understand American movies just as well as German ones.

Given Ernst's relative social isolation in Lodi, it's understandable that movies played an important role for him during this time, as well as for Amalie to some extent.

September 15, 1948

Last Saturday I saw a wonderful film called Foreign Affairs. *Please let me know if this movie is also showing where you are; if not, I'd really like to tell you a little about it. The plot actually takes place in today's Berlin.*

October 1, 1948

Since Tuesday I've spent every evening this week in the cinema, which makes it high time for me to write to my darling. Of course, you'll say right away that I must have quite a lot of money to go to the movies, but these were films that I simply couldn't resist. Just imagine: a German film called The Musicians *was shown in Lodi. Even weeks before it came to town I was looking forward to it, because it's been more than two years since I'd seen a film in the German language. And so—even though I'd already seen this movie in Germany—I went out with my mother last Tuesday. I'd only been in the cinema for a few minutes when I felt peculiar, because German was being spoken from the screen. I didn't feel homesick; instead, everything seemed so strange to me...I could hardly concentrate at all, and I kept on asking myself what I found so disappointing. I do, of course, speak German every day, and I didn't believe at all that I could ever forget this language. I was ashamed of myself, but I couldn't help myself, because when, for example, Paul Horbiger makes his marriage proposal, etc., none of this seemed realistic to me. But then suddenly, inspired by the atmospheric music of the Biergarten, I liked it, and when Hans Moser started to say things like "I could care less" ["Alles ist mir Wurst"] and "fool and numbskull"["Deppe und Dickschädel"] then I really started to enjoy the film. Only then did I really feel at home again, and I thought that it had now been well over two years that anyone has angrily called me a "Deppen" in German. Finally, I was so happy that I stayed in my seat until the second showing ended. I went to the cinema again on Wednesday, and now I'm in seventh heaven because I was able to watch a German film once again. As far as the language itself is concerned, one thing I learned was that I now understand American movies just as well as German ones. Actually speaking and writing in English, though, is still something that I can't do all that well.*

Yesterday I was at the movies again. It was a new American film called <u>Berlin Express.</u> It's a story about today's Germany, and actually it's pretty good. Especially interesting is the fact that this film is not just in English, but also in German, French, and Russian. So, for example, the American officials speak English, the Americans speak broken German to their German girlfriends—or these young women speak poor English with them in turn; German business people, etc., speak German; at the same time the French officials speak French at the train station in Paris. During a scene in a black market people are speaking gibberish. I'd guess that about thirty-five percent was in German, and I just can't imagine how someone who only knew English could make sense of it all.

When we grew up in the Sixties, we rarely went to the movies, and when we went as an entire family it was serious business, far from mere entertainment. Just like the opera or ballet performances that our parents selected, the films they brought us to often held a moral or educational element that they wanted to impress upon us. Once my father drove Tom and me over to downtown Stockton to see an evening showing of *Doctor Zhivago*, and it was clear from his no-nonsense demeanor that this was not just intended to be a fun time or a trivial diversion. Both my parents had already seen the film, and I suspect that they wanted us to get familiar with it because, in an oblique way, it presented a picture of what they'd experienced in their younger years—a world of social turmoil and disruption, of privation and struggle, of individuals determined to survive in dark and difficult times.

Even though the Catholic Church officially frowned upon *2001: A Space Odyssey*, our dad—who had remained a devout churchgoer in spite of the disruptions of Vatican II—insisted that we all pile into the family car and head up to a Sacramento cinema when it first opened up. At that point he'd already started work at Aerojet General in Rancho Cordova, and taking us to that film was his way of giving us a sense of what his work involved, of the visions that he and his colleagues pursued and tried to make real. Among other projects, he was involved in the NERVA program, which aimed to launch a manned mission to Mars until the effort was discontinued in 1973.

On the other hand, a handful of our movie outings were meant for pleasure and nothing but pleasure. In the late Sixties Tom and I saw a James Bond double feature at the cinema on Lodi Avenue—*Thunderball* and *You Only Live Twice*—and soon after we talked our dad into seeing the same double bill with us in a drive-in movie theater along West Lane between Lodi and Stockton.

All three of us were entranced with the smooth, confident heroism of Sean Connery, the exotic scenery, the edge-of-your-seat car chases, and—of course—the array of nifty gadgets.

For a while after that Bond films were something that "the men" in the family often went to whenever possible. When *Diamonds Are Forever* premiered in the early Seventies, my father and I stood in a long line at the cinema in downtown Stockton to check it out immediately. We also checked out *The Spy Who Loved Me* a few years later, and stayed in our seats after the final credits were over and waited for a while in the semi-darkness so that we could check out the opening ski chase sequence a second time at the start of the next showing.

Watching Bond movies and reading several of the Fleming novels—not to mention relishing Sixties television fare such as *Mission: Impossible* and *It Takes a Thief*—led me to wonder on occasion what our father had actually done during his stint with U.S. Army intelligence in postwar Berlin. My imagination conjured up various far-fetched scenarios, and it didn't settle down when, again and again, he refused to tell me anything about that time in his life when I broached the subject. The suspicion that he'd done his own bit of derring-do back in the day stayed with me for years, spurred in part by some of his curious habits. For example, about once a month it seemed that he'd get a fire going in the living room fireplace and then feed papers into the flames, destroying them thoroughly and systematically. To my youthful mind actions like those seemed to match the behavior of a former spy.

Here where we are the most beautiful theatrical works are already being performed once again.

To judge from her letters, Liselotte was far less enamored of the movies. Plays and music, and especially music as spectacle—opera and ballet—clearly held sway at the center of her life.

April 28, 1947

Does Lodi have a theater and a cinema? In Munich it's the busiest time right now for places like these. The opera house, state operetta house, the theater, and so many other locations are now doing a brisk business. I really enjoy going to the theater, most of all to see classical plays. Unfortunately you never can get tickets for the opera. I've only been there twice, and that was just because of lucky breaks. Can you also hear the Swiss radio station? That also always has pretty music, also in German; we often listen to it.

June 26, 1947

Yesterday I was in the theater again, in the Schauspielhaus. The performance was very good. I personally think it's awful that there's no theater in Lodi, and that you're not able to afford something like that. But I think you can enjoy yourself on your excursions. It doesn't always have to be going to the theater.

Apparently ticket prices were within her reach, allowing her to attend live performances fairly regularly.

July 23, 1947

Yesterday I was in the theater. An old Bavarian play from the year 1740. The traditional costumes and the music were splendid. Are you familiar with the old instruments, such as the dulcimer and the many others that you usually can't even hear anymore? Here where we are the most beautiful plays are already being performed once again. I really like to go, and actually I also go often. Other than that I can't buy much, or anything at all; this way I at least have the pleasure, and at the same time the wonderful change of pace after work.

Right now many American films are showing here. All in all, I'm not very enthused about them, and I don't go to them very often.

Sometimes the dangers of postwar Munich prevented her from indulging in this pastime. On January 10, 1948 she wrote that *I haven't gone to the theater in quite a while because it isn't safe on the streets here anymore.* In spite of that, though, she mentioned in the same letter that *I saw an afternoon performance of Schubert's <u>Blossom Time</u>.*

Important for Liselotte was the theatrical as well as the musical— the intricate scenery on stage, the thespian expertise of the singers, and—of course—the quality of the costumes.

February 27, 1948

Yesterday I was in the opera house to see an evening of ballet. You know, it was beautiful. It was so magnificent that it can't even be described! The costumes and the dancers' performances—simply unique! It's too bad that you always have a lot of trouble getting tickets!

During this time, just as she did decades later when our family attended operas in San Francisco, she took the trials and tragic fates of operatic characters very much to heart. Madame Butterfly always provoked an especially powerful response from her.

March 9, 1948

Last Friday I went to the opera again. It was Puccini's <u>Madame Butterfly</u>! You know, the music was simply wonderful; it was so lovely that I was just entranced! Remember the acquaintance of mine that I told you about the last time? He got the tickets. We sat in a private box among a lot of Americans. They didn't know that we were Germans, because it's not necessary that they find out the Germans are also still able to sit in such places. At any rate, the production was magnificent. A guest tenor from Italy was there. Can you imagine how well he sang? The opera itself is somewhat sad, and I had to cry a little even though I tried to control myself, but the work ends tragically: Madame Butterfly commits hari-kari on the stage! It's downright eerie, but also beautiful!

For Liselotte, opera was never a laughing matter—not even comedies like Donizetti's *The Daughter of the Regiment*. Every facet of such a work—from the characters' yearnings and passions to the conductor's movements and the strains of the orchestra—had to be taken seriously, and they all were. When Liselotte prepared us children for an upcoming operatic performance, it was as if she telling us about real flesh-and-blood people. Not just Madame Butterfly, but also Otello, Lucia di Lammermoor, Aida—each of them lived and breathed for her, and under the spell of her words and her limitless enthusiasm we came to see them that way as well.

Beyond the giddy spectacle of an operatic performance itself, the posh ambience of an opera house itself appealed to Liselotte, filled as it typically was with well-dressed patrons.

Oct. 3, 1948

Now to a completely different subject. Yesterday your Liselotte was dressed up as an "elegant woman"—that's not me saying that, but rather some other people in the house, and not Miss Reiner—and I went to the opera house to see <u>Carmen</u>. It was just magnificent—this music, and the stage designs and the costumes—once again up to the standards of peace time. The clothing of those in the attendance—now long evening clothes once again—was also splendid, and of course these distinguished people come with their cars because that sort of clothing would look very odd in the streetcar. But I still saw some things that didn't appeal to me and that I myself wouldn't want to put on. I was wearing something up-to-date—a long wine-red dress, completely smooth and made simply, just with a large taffeta ribbon that was tied on the back. It's actually silly when I describe it this way, because you can't see it and maybe you're not interested in it all that much.

January 9, 1949

On Thursday, Epiphany, I went to a large concert in a private home. It was very lovely—many very elegant people who were going on forty years of age, and everything presented in candlelight. This time Miss Reiner also came along, so this time at least I wasn't alone. This Thursday I'll be able to go to the opera—it's a present—to see <u>The Magic Bullet</u>. *I'm already really looking forward to it. I hope that it's not as foggy as it was the last time.*

Hermann John accompanied her to such musical events many times.

January 15, 1951

Yesterday afternoon I was in the Gärtnerplatz Theater to see Carl Zeller's <u>The Bird Seller</u>. *H.J. was with me.*

Here she only makes a terse reference to Herr John, probably not dwelling too much on that point so as not to upset Ernst.

It was very nice—above all the music—but unfortunately the audience wasn't that good. That's always painful for me, because I do really like seeing well-dressed people. For me that makes for an elevated, festive atmosphere.

Given her fascination with the stage trappings of opera, it's not surprising that she was also drawn to the visual arts.

June 30, 1948

My dear Ernst! You know from the letter that I wrote yesterday that I'm now on vacation and that the weather is terrible. This afternoon I'll go into the city and possibly walk through an art gallery.

Ernst's social life in Lodi seems to have been fairly limited and modest. Liselotte's, by contrast, included an impressive share of parties and other social events.

July 23, 1947

Last Saturday I was out in the country. I helped out with the harvest, but of course it was more laughing and fun and games than serious work. But for once it was something completely different, and it was very nice. In the evening we then went out to dance. You know, all of the old folk dances like the country waltz, the Rheinländer, the polka, etc.—also the Schuhplattler—require a certain formation. It was really very nice. I went back home early on Sunday morning. Do people also dance where you are?

Sept. 8, 1947

On August 23ʳᵈ I went to a dance evening with traditional costumes. You know, it was really nice. There I could see, for the first time, the old folk dances being performed in the traditional costumes of Tölz, Dachau, Lengries, Dorfen, etc.—but everyone one of them is distinct. Afterwards there was a dance for the general public, but here there were just polkas, Rheinländer, and other such beautiful dances, because those dressed in costumes are not allowed to dance anything else, but that was of course the least important thing about the whole festival.

When the prince comes, I'll need to let his royal highness give me a Fasching kiss…

Liselotte also came to relish the carnival season, known as *Fasching* in southern Germany, probably for the same reason that she enjoyed the bustle and pomp of an opera house foyer—it gave her as well as those around her the chance to dress up in a way that transcended the grim challenges of the everyday.

During 1948, though, the conditions of her life compelled her to refrain from taking part in the season's programmed craziness.

January 10, 1948

Today Fasching started here—naturally, and unfortunately, it's not the type of Fasching that we used to have; otherwise I'd take part in it, because I really like things like that. But in the circumstances that we have now it's not pleasant. That makes me very sad, because I've never actually experienced a real Fasching. How does this look where you are? Does it exist over there?

The next year she could participate in the festivities as fully as she'd wanted.

January 9, 1949

This year there'll be a large Fasching celebration that runs until the first of March. I really want to take part in an actual Fasching because up to now

I've never had the chance to do so, but I think that I personally won't be able to attend very many events. For quite a while now I've wanted to go dancing again—but really go dancing. The newspaper has already reported about an incredible number of public balls, above all in the Museum of German Art, in the silver hall of the German Theater, etc. Where you are I'm sure Fasching is also being celebrated—are there also grand balls where you are? Will your firm have a company ball? We won't have one at ours; I also wouldn't be very interested in that. Where you are, are there things like dance courses?

Fasching festivities, it seems, were never complete without the presence of sham royalty to preside over various balls—and Liselotte soon got the opportunity to fill one of these honored positions herself.

January 14, 1950

Now to deal with another topic. Today I got the news in writing, though I hadn't known about this at all. I've been selected to be the "Queen of the Ball" of the city's Elecktro Guild. I was completely caught off guard and wondered if it was really true. When the prince comes, I'll need to let his royal highness give me a Fasching kiss, and of course I'll need to dance the first waltz with him. At any rate I'll have to be the first at the front, right behind the dance instructor leading the polonaise, and then I'll dance a solo waltz with the first master of the guild, and later on I'll dance with other distinguished gentlemen. Of course, at the very beginning, when I'm greeted, I'll be given wonderful roses, etc. All of this will happen on February 17th in the newly constructed Augustiner Cellar. This means that I'll have to go to the Valenci dance studio right away to learn all of the new dances—because it'd be ridiculous for me to be the Queen of the Ball and not be familiar with them.

A few days later Liselotte continued writing the same letter.

Well, yesterday I had the first dance lesson at Valenci. It was really very nice. There was such a buoyant atmosphere there, the kind that you can only find at Valenci. My instructor was very concerned that two men had asked me dance by the time he looked around. I just had to laugh when that happened. We danced a very authentic "polonaise." Then we learned different elements of Fasching dances, etc. Then we danced the samba—that's really lovely when

*it's danced the way that we learned it. The evening ended at around 10:15
PM, and at 10:30 PM I was already at home. That was really great.*

Fasching took center stage in her life once again a year later.

January 15, 1951

*By the way, it's been said that this year's royal couple (Prince Charles II
and Grete) looks very attractive. On Friday I'll actually see them in person!*

When I studied in Germany at the state universities in Freiburg
and Tübingen, the initial thrill and novelty of Fasching quickly wore
off for me, and the season's colorful antics and socially mandated
silliness became more of a nuisance than anything else. Liselotte's
fascination with these traditions never flagged, however—with one
apparent exception.

January 28, 1951

*The Fasching parade will take place next Saturday. I don't know for sure
if I'll go to see it. Last year it actually wasn't supposed to have been all that
special. You know, it had a lot of advertisements.*

In this year she also made it a point to attend several large-scale
Fasching events.

January 28, 1951

*My dear Ernst! To begin with, I want to let you know that I didn't get
to bed last night at all; instead I was able to go to one of the most beautiful
Fasching parties in Munich, the Festival of the Jugglers in the Löwenbräu
Cellar. I hope that you understand that it was Fasching and that because of
this I started saying "du" with H. J. [Hermann John]. During the Fasching
season everything says "du" [the casual form of address] to everyone
else. This evening I didn't say it when I was talking to a man in a stylish
"Münchhausen" mask, and before I knew it—I didn't have a chance—he
gave me a "brotherhood kiss."*

Such a kiss signified that they'd now address each other informally.

And so for that reason a person should always use "du" right away from the start; otherwise there'll be lots of "brotherhood kisses"! My dear Ernst! H. J. wouldn't have done that on his own, but Miss Reiner, my parents… actually everyone said that it's ridiculous for us to address each other formally and then say "du" to our friends. Mr. J. didn't have it all that easy with me. When the two of us weren't dancing, I was still on the dance floor, because men I didn't know asked me to dance. Once he wanted to bring me back to our table, but before he knew it, someone had already asked me to dance, and so Mr. John was left to go back to our table alone. That's why I was just amazed about the many different dance partners that I had—men I didn't even know—because various young women were there alone and they had no partners. The music played from seven in the evening until seven in the morning. I was back home again on January 28th. The jugglers—itinerant circus performers…gave a presentation, and the best talents of the Zirkus Krone were on hand. I tell you, the atmosphere was wonderful. You can't imagine how much fun something like that can be. Please, my dear Ernst, please don't be upset with me, but you can understand that after you've danced your way through a full night you can't write all that legibly. Please understand that, won't you? I haven't slept yet, in fact. Next Friday I'm set to go to another lovely ball. I'll go there dressed as a knight's page; I've borrowed the costume. Later on I'll give you a complete report about it. On February 7th this year's Fasching will already be over.

February 9, 1951

During Fasching I had a whole set of Christian names; naturally that was just for Fasching, and they were only valid during Fasching. Mr. John always had to laugh when I listed all of the names for him, and he thought it would have been better had I been given numbers.

The photo albums contain a few dozen pictures that show these balls as well as Liselotte's preparations for them—all of them painstakingly organized and captioned. Just as the ski photos documented Ernst's enthusiasm for the mountains, these pictures show her capacity to cultivate an enviable life-affirming stance in the face of the troubles and challenges that confronted her.

When I read it, I soon have to start crying, and then I'm ashamed of myself…

At the end of my first-grade year at St. Anne's School my teacher, a Dominican nun, gave me the "Bookworm Award." It was a prize for having read the most books—fifty in total—during the term. These were in English, of course, a language that I was still wrestling with. I owe my own love of books—not to mention my affection for all bookstores grand and small—to both of my parents.

Liselotte's taste in novels revealed her interest in other cultures and historical periods.

March 2, 1947

I'm actually reading about the Gold Rush in California right now; it's a novel by Zane Grey called <u>The Border Legion</u>. It's extremely interesting, very exciting and suspenseful, but also very well written. The entire plot takes place in the mountains. It might even be that the area where you live now is described in this book. Since I'm now talking about books…<u>Gone with the Wind</u> also takes place in America, and parts of it deal with Gold Rush in California and battles in Mexico. It's set in the era following the Civil War, approximately after 1863. I've just finished reading it. It was very good, and above all it taught me a lot about history. By chance, do you know the book by "Caldwell, Taylor"—<u>Einst wird kommen der Tag</u>?

The original English title of Taylor Caldwell's novel is *Dynasty of Death*. A Reader's Digest version—in German—always sat on a bookshelf next to our mother's "reading chair" in the corner of our living room.

The Caldwell novel—which my father wound up reading as well—made a strong impact on both of them, and given their rave reviews I checked out the original English version and went through it during my high school years. As in the case of *Doctor Zhivago*, its plot—a sprawling multigenerational family saga centering on an arms manufacturer named Joseph Barbour—touched indirectly on some of their experiences during the war and the lessons that they'd drawn from those experiences.

Around this time Liselotte must have also read *The Treasure of Silver Lake*, a novel by Karl May, a prolific nineteenth- and early twentieth-century writer of adventure novels for the young and young at heart. Later on, when she and Ernst lived in California, they both took a road trip to Silver Lake, and Liselotte was astonished to discover that May's description of that body of water was dead on.

March 2, 1948

You know, I'm now the librarian in the firm where I work. That means that I have to manage the workplace library—which contains more than six hundred books—and check them out, etc. This adds up to quite a bit of work on the side, but I really enjoy doing this sort of activity, and because of it I'm reading an awful lot, because I need to know what the books that I'm checking out are about. Of course, I haven't read all of them by a long shot—it'd be a big exaggeration to say that—but I do already know some of these books! I've been filling this position since I came to this firm!

Later on in her life, after all four of us children had grown up, Lisa would reprise this role at the Lodi Public Library for a time and then subsequently, for several years, at St. Anne's School. Both positions reinforced her fascination with the world of the written word.

Just as in the opera house, Liselotte deeply absorbed the inner life of the characters she read about and made their struggles and trials her own. Tragic, heart-wrenching scenes in novels often brought forth the same reaction from her as operatic situations did, and she sometimes spoke to us about fictional characters as if they were very much alive.

May 16, 1948

Now I'm reading a wonderful book called <u>The Meterologist</u> by Heer; unfortunately it's very sad. When I read it, I soon have to start crying, and *then I'm ashamed of myself, but I just can't help it. But the book deals with real life, not some fantasy of a life as you read about so often. You're not going to make fun of me, are you?*

In the autumn of 2006 our mother underwent eye surgery to treat glaucoma and cataracts; upon her recovery she took advantage of her regained vision to go on a robust reading binge. After looking over the bookshelves in my living room, she landed on Somerset Maughm's *Of Human Bondage*, borrowed it for a time, and went through all of its six hundred pages. Of course, she wasn't without her criticisms of Philip Carey, the novel's protagonist. "I'm reading the chapters when he's living in Paris," she reported to me once on the phone, "and, I must say, I'm very disappointed with him." Apparently Philip's new circle of friends and acquaintances didn't suit her in the least, and after that he never found his way back into her good graces.

During this phase of his life Ernst concentrated on scientific and technical material, but later on his reading interests transcended the titles he needed for professional advancement. Paperbacks on his shelves in Lodi included works by philosophers like Kant and Schopenhauer as well as several extensively highlighted books by the psychoanalyst Erich Fromm, including *The Sane Society*. Just as he sought to garner a more extensive understanding of engineering for his work at Super Mold and, later, at Aerojet General, so too he struggled later on to get a better handle on such areas as history—in particular the history of the Jewish people—and philosophy.

His profession, though, was always a crucial part of his life.

CHAPTER FOUR

Work

Constructing things is my passion, and for me it's almost a necessity.

A surprising amount of our parents' correspondence related to their experiences on the job. While Ernst stayed put at Super Mold during these years, Liselotte found employment at several firms.

Ernst devoted most of his time and energy to his work, something that paid dividends in terms of the rewarding challenges that it brought his way and the recognition that he eventually received. He was clearly gratified to have landed a job that matched his intellectual leanings.

April 12, 1947

Now I also want to tell you something about myself. Even though I'm really homesick a lot of the time, in other ways things are going well with me so far. My work brings me contentment. Constructing things is my passion, and for me it's almost a necessity. You know that, of course.

November 4, 1947

Today I really had a lot of things to do at work, and I had to deal with several nagging problems. But I always look forward to the next day of work, and I hope to wrap up each task successfully...I love my job a lot and I hope that I can also get some work that I can do independently at home. Until now, though, I still haven't had any luck.

September 9, 1948

Today it was yet another exciting day at work. I was in the shop almost constantly to get my machine to work for the exhibit. Even though I'm actually only supposed to supervise, usually I work along with the others so that we can be certain of success. The foremen and the mechanics always support me, which really pleases me, especially when I sometimes have to deal with envious colleagues. You know, a lot of the time these people are conceited, and the workers get angry about that. A few days ago I made a bad mistake, and I was ready to admit to it, because an expensive casting piece had been ruined. At that point the carpenter responsible for making models came and put together a new one right away, and the new casting was ready in one-and-a-half days, and we could avoid further unpleasantries. The workers in the machine shop also do their best; all of them want to help the [in English] *German boy.* [in German] *Something like that really makes me happy.*

In addition to Super Mold, he did work in his apartment to earn some extra income.

October 17, 1948

It's already eleven at night, but still I don't want to—and I can't—keep from sending a few more friendly words to you. I'm writing this to you on my drawing board because at the moment pretty much all I'm doing is working here. While I'm always under pressure to complete the drawings for an injection molding machine, my free time is filled with constructing the mechanism for a sausage sandwich machine—that is, a small commission I'm doing at home.

In the Sixties and Seventies, while we sprawled on the living room carpet and absorbed the likes of *Gilligan's Island* and *I Dream of Jeannie*, our dad would more often than not be working away at his desk in the corner. As a rule, he could tune out the dialogue, atmospheric background music, and commercial interruptions as he fulfilled his tasks, but not always. Once, during an especially fascinating and gruesome installment of Rod Serling's *Night Gallery*, he shuddered noticeably and then insisted that I turn the TV off. I had no choice but to honor his request, and to this day I still don't know what happened to Bill Bixby at the end of that particular episode.

Ernst put in long hours at his firm as a matter of routine.

November 28, 1948

Right now I'm working every Saturday morning; the rest of the firm, however, is quiet on Saturday and Sunday. Personally, I don't mind—quite the contrary. You wanted to know about the machine of mine that was at the exhibition. Thanks for asking. Everything is really okay; at least I didn't have to put up with any negative criticism or unfavorable remarks—outside of the machine's price, anyway. I can't really complain about my job; after all, there'll be small irritations everywhere.

His work load at Super Mold never seemed to get smaller.

March 17, 1950

My dear Liselotte!

I hope that you're really doing well, and I can report the same about myself. At my job the amount of work hasn't dropped off, but at the same time I've got as many irritating things to deal with as before. Sometimes it seems that these are an integral part of my job, something that I'm being paid for. And so I hardly get anything else done, because I often spend up to twelve hours at work, and all I do there is make calculations, check over drawings, and work out my ideas.

Liselotte supported his efforts, and many times she praised his zeal and dedication.

October 19, 1946

This morning I was really happy and surprised to get your letter. I've already found out where you are now from Miss Reiner and Miss Gödrer. You and I really never would have imagined that we'd ever come to be so far away from each other. But the main thing is that things are going fairly well for you. As time passes, you'll certainly rise in the ranks, because you can show your talents and your abilities a lot better after you've gotten used to your job there. I hear from Miss Reiner that you have to relearn all of the measurements; that's quite a bit. Anyway, I send you all of my best wishes for the future.

March 17, 1947

I'm really glad that you're having such luck in your career, because that's the only way that you'll be able to get ahead. Of course, you'll have to work a lot and accomplish a lot. But the main thing is that you enjoy it.

October 5, 1947

You know, I'm not worried about your career, because I know that you have impressive skills.

A few years later, when Ernst wrote his "soldier letters" to her, she kept encouraging him about his position at Super Mold.

February 9, 1951

They miss you in your firm; that's a very good sign—above all, also for later, when you can get back to your career. It would be a big advantage if you could get your old job back. Over here that was usually the case, but I don't know if it works that way where you are.

The firm is a lot bigger than the Reiner family's company, and it's also very interesting...

Late in 1946 Liselotte left Therese Reiner's firm and found office work elsewhere.

October 19, 1946

Can you believe it, dear Roesch? I would have so much to write about that I really don't know where I should actually begin. You know, it all has to do with me personally. All right, here goes. Since January 1946 I'm no longer working in the Reiner Company. Dr. Gademann wanted an older bookkeeper, and for that reason it was better that I left. However, I still live in Miss Reiner's house—since a bomb hit my living quarters—which I suspect isn't exactly the best arrangement now and then. But that can't be changed for the time being, because I don't have a room for myself at home; there's no place there for me right now. Since April 15, 1946, I've been working as a bookkeeper in the English fuel and oil company "Runo-Everth." The firm is a lot bigger than the Reiner family's company, and it's also very interesting. For a while now we've had contact with England, and so now and then there's something to read or write in English.

Like Ernst, Liselotte tended to express contentment and gratitude about the job that she'd found. Her letters often emphasized the benefits and advantages that her new firm had to offer.

January 22, 1947

At work they put together a really pretty birthday poem for me, half of it in German and half in English. Besides that, they also gave me apples, etc. for presents, and even Lore-Lies went out of her way for me. She phoned the firm, but I wasn't there—I'd taken some time off—and so she had to call here, and then she wished me a Happy Birthday in a very sweet way. All in all, it was very nice, and I have nothing to complain about. At work, as of the beginning of the New Year and then subsequently on my birthday, I got a pay raise that amounts to twenty-five percent of my current salary; that's also very nice.

January 1, 1948

A short time ago I wrote to you about the Christmas celebration at the firm. You know, it really turned out well, in spite of its modest trappings. Everyone was delighted with the music that I played, or anyway at least that's what they told me. I also recited a poem.

The superior time management skills that our mother displayed when raising us were already in evidence in the late Forties.

July 23, 1947

There's something that I wanted to tell you about most of all. Dear Ernst, you can't imagine where and how I'm writing this letter. Right now, in fact, my lunch break has started, and I took a chair along with me and set it down in a corner of our storage area. So I ask that you forgive this shaky handwriting. In these circumstances you'll have to work a little harder to read this. But, you know, this evening I have to go school again, and each day passes by this way, and then I still haven't written to you. Today's a magnificent day; it's really sad to be sitting in an office. But what can you really do? It's going very well for me at work.

Despite her general satisfaction with the job Liselotte yearned to pursue more work opportunities for herself, primarily by acquiring more languages.

March 17, 1947

My work situation is actually also very good. Of all of the women working there, I'm the youngest bookkeeper, and it means a lot when the "older bookkeepers" have to admit this fact and not just treat me as a "bookkeeping assistant"—as they'd very much want to. But I don't want do this type of work for the long haul, because I want to use my language abilities somehow. You see, I'm actually learning more English now, and besides that I'm taking Spanish lessons and then also some French. Now I'll just wait and see what develops. I hope that I'm not learning all of this for nothing. Time passes by so quickly, and I'm convinced that if you learn something in your spare time then at least you're using that time well.

At one point she weighed the pros and cons of working for American employers.

June 11, 1947

Do you still have to learn more—math or something else—for your line of work? Are you still learning more English, or do you get enough practice at work? I've already thought a few times about applying for a job with the Americans, but then I always decided against it because dealing with them is a bit tricky, in a way. You can imagine it for yourself, and for that reason I just don't want to apply for such positions. I've often thought that I've now gotten some training in the language, and they pay comparatively very well—of course the pay is never that great in a private firm. Besides that, if I worked for the Americans I'd be able to get food without using stamps. But I'm not thinking seriously anymore about doing this. I think that, when all is said and done, the people at home wouldn't let me do it.

Just yesterday evening I got another lecture from the second bookkeeper.

More often than not our parents were reticent and stoical when it came to challenges on the job; they rarely betrayed the work-related stress and anxiety that sometimes took their toll on them. And so it was surprising for me to find out about some of the discomforting and stressful work situations that had come their way earlier.

Liselotte had to deal with some troublesome personalities at her workplaces, and Ernst did his best to console her and buck her up.

April 12, 1947

I hope that your old colleagues at work don't bring you down. They must be some really irritating characters. But, if being envious makes them happy, just let them have their fun.

He also gave his two cents' worth of advice about her options for the coming years.

November 4, 1947

All right, so you don't want to come to America. Depending on the circumstances, I don't think it'd be impossible for me to arrange for you to come over here. But how can this benefit you if you don't want to come to me, but go to Switzerland instead? If you have a career opportunity, then my advice to you is to go to Switzerland, because it's very beautiful there. (That's what I've heard, at least.)

Liselotte continued to nurture a positive outlook about her work situation in spite of ongoing issues with some of her co-workers and one of her superiors in particular.

December 13, 1947

I have to get upset now and then at work. Just yesterday evening I got another lecture from the second bookkeeper. She's asked that I don't always leave so punctually in the evening because that doesn't make a good impression, but in the future I'll still leave as I've done up to now. Sometimes I really have to put up with quite a bit from my female colleagues. I do actually like working in this office because it's within walking distance and I don't need to take the awful streetcars. But I often hope that things will be different someday. Things aren't bad for me at work as far as my work itself is concerned, but often the way I'm treated isn't nice because, of course, I'm the youngest one there. Now, for sure, I'll wait until the winter is over, and then I'll see what I can do. But a more favorable position, something better, will come along.

Later on a visitor from England precipitated a whole new set of disruptions and challenges at her firm.

February 27, 1948

At work right now we have a lot to do. A director from London has come to visit, and he'll be staying for fourteen days. The work is very interesting; I've already written memorandums for him. They're still in German, but he dictates with a foreign accent, and I was allowed to translate my first "letters" (not very short ones) from English into German. I succeeded pretty well; still, I had to rush. I didn't have much time to complete the job! At least that makes the otherwise uncomfortable things at work somewhat more palatable. Our boss is actually so agitated that she doesn't even know herself anymore. When I deal with this "boss," I remain perfectly calm; they can't rob me of that.

March 9, 1948

My English boss has now gone again. On the one hand that's nice, because it was very stressful for me. He always dictated to me, and I had an incredible amount of work. Please excuse my messy handwriting today, but at work today I had to write so much—and write it all so quickly—that my wrists and especially my fingers hurt right now…But, you know, since my letters take such a long time to get to you, I wanted to write to you right away. I hope that you can read my words!

But your "pleasant" boss apparently isn't the type to recognize your worth.

Liselotte likewise supported Ernst when he opened up about his trials on the job, inviting him to share more about his frustrations at Super Mold.

June 26, 1947

I'm always happy to hear that things are going well for you in your career. Except…what I don't completely understand in your letter is the way that you sigh: "Sometimes it gets on my nerves!" Do you have so much to do? If it's not that, then what's the problem?

She also started to voice her irritation about Ernst's boss, who to her mind didn't adequately value his contributions to the company.

July 23, 1947

I'm always happy when you tell about your career, most of all because you've found so much success. Hopefully your boss also values your achievements—or what does he think about it, I mean when it comes to your salary? I was really shocked when I read about the dentist's bill for 130 dollars in your letter. That's really awful! I imagine that it must be terrible when someone gets sick in America—without health insurance.

Liselotte also counseled him to make sure that he had enough down time, enough leisure hours away from the pressure of the work environment.

September 8, 1947

I'm glad that things are always going well with you, at least somewhat well. Based on what I've found out here, living must be fairly expensive where you are. In my last letter I already wrote you that you shouldn't just work more in case you really do have a drafting table at home now. In the evenings it'd definitely be better for you to relax, or read, or do something else. But your "pleasant" boss apparently isn't the type to recognize your worth. Just waiting patiently won't bring you anything. I especially want to stress that you don't have to send me any special shipments, because I don't want that. It's better if you don't work for such long hours, so that you yourself benefit from your hard work.

Similar exhortations cropped up in some of her later letters.

February 2, 1949

You always have so much work to do. Ten hours per day, and even more than that, that's really very long. I'm always a little afraid that you're working yourself too hard, given how busy you are.

The "dad" we knew as we grew up could be good-natured and boyish, or—on various occasions, and without much warning—he could be volatile, and his fierce temper would then erupt with a vengeance. During the late Forties circumstances at Super Mold sometimes aroused his exasperation and his ire.

December 3, 1947

Today I really had to get upset again at work. You should hear me once when I yell and swear in English.

Apparently he started using more profanity in the States than he had earlier on.

October 20, 1948

Please don't be scared about the swear words that I mentioned. I was exaggerating there a little. To give you an example, it's like this. When a threaded nut just doesn't fit the way it's supposed to, then two years ago I would have said something like, [in English] *"This nut is not good."* [in German] *Now, though, I've adopted the American approach, and I might say,* [in English] *"That damn nut doesn't fit."* [in German] *I don't even know myself why I've actually written about this; I hope that you're not uncomfortable about this and disappointed with me.*

You know, Bauer is just like the ones here.

Liselotte felt strongly that Ernst had merited a raise many times over, but he still hadn't gotten one, and this issue became a leitmotif in their correspondence. In her mind Ernst definitely deserved more money because of the machines that he was designing and building for Super Mold.

The cover of a company publication from these years even showcased Ernst standing in front of one of these contraptions.

January 22, 1947

It's really too bad that you still haven't received your pay raise, that your boss can be so tough. You already earned it a long time ago. Maybe they want to spend their money prudently, but they also need your abilities and your knowledge. I'm really eager to find out when you finally do get your raise. I'm absolutely convinced that your machine will work well, because how could you suddenly make a mistake, as you put it? That can't be; that just doesn't happen so easily for someone like you.

Ernst dutifully recounted the progress he'd made on these projects.

November 4, 1947

I think I've already told you that one of my machines would be sent to an exhibit. In the meantime all of that's already happened, and I was successful. My machine was judged to be one of the best ones there. Just imagine: my boss "promised" to give me a pay raise; well, that's something, anyway.

The mention of a mere promise hardly mollified Liselotte.

December 13, 1947

What's going on with your boss? Has he given you that pay raise in the meantime— the one he promised you once and that you've deserved for quite a while? You know, if he hasn't, then it'd be high time for him to do so. Have you been able to pay off your dentist's bill already?

January 6, 1948

I'll keep my fingers crossed again for your machine; I hope it works. But certainly it'll work, because you're not making any mistakes. I can really imagine how important it is for you, because so much depends on it— maybe, at long last, you'll get your pay raise?!? This boss of yours! If he knew that I was always agitating against him…but it's really irritating when he doesn't do what he promised he would and give you what you deserve. You know, Bauer [the name of Ernst's boss] *is just like the ones here. They make promises and agree to things, and then they don't pay; so, in that sense, they're the same sort of people. I completely understand your thoughts about work conditions and career possibilities because I can readily believe that a person devotes himself to his work more fully when he's living in a faraway place as opposed to living in his homeland. That's already true because you're labeled as "being German," as you yourself mention.*

At long last Mr. Bauer came through.

January 30, 1948

Just imagine—today I got the long-promised pay raise. I'm now pulling in exactly twice as much as I did one-and-a-half years ago when I worked in New York as a manual laborer.

Liselotte lost no time in sharing her delight at the news.

February 7, 1948

Congratulations! You got a pay raise! My dear Ernst! Congratulations on your success. I'm so happy for you, happy that your boss has finally recognized your outstanding achievements, and above all it's a new incentive for you when you see that your work is paying off, because you already earned this raise a long time ago. When I think about this over and over, that you achieved this in a country in which the language and the measurements and so many related things were all completely foreign to you, then my amazement and admiration know no bounds. And you've made so much progress in such a very short span of time! I also wish with all of my heart that you'll always have success in your career, because that's very important. Because one's often heard about very intelligent people who can't get very far in their careers even though they try hard. So, once again, good luck!

One apparatus that Ernst had designed was finally completed and put to the test.

February 16, 1948

By the way, the big machine of mine is working. You should have seen this—how it worked while a crowd of people (all of them pessimists) were watching. And, in spite of that, it was a success and there was a general amazement. I'm in seventh heaven.

Liselotte was quick to respond with jubilant approbation.

February 27, 1948

When I think about your success with the new machine, I'm really happy. Accept my warmest and deepest congratulations regarding your success! I wish with all of my heart that things always go so well with all of your work! They must have been amazed, right? Especially since most of them were pessimists. What does your boss say about it? And you'll be happy—right, dear Ernst—because it's really nerve-wracking until the machine is completely finished and it actually functions. Well, once again I wish you much, much luck with your work, because that's the most important thing; otherwise a person can't get ahead and get recognition even if he has a lot of knowledge and intelligence...And you're building a new one again. What sort of machine are you constructing?

Our mother always took an interest in all of our pursuits—in Barbara's Japanese, Ursula's progress at Humphrey's Business College, Tom's pre-med courses and subsequent medical training, and my plunge into German sociology when I was completing some translation projects. Here she showed the same level of curiosity about Ernst's contraptions.

March 9, 1948

Today, above all, I want to find out what sort of machines you're building so that I can get a sense of what they're like. Please tell me about them in more detail; I'm immensely interested in them. It's really great that you were successful with your last difficult project! I always have to admire the way that you're able to accomplish this in a foreign country...Do you actually have a long workday? Here you hear that people only work until four o'clock in America! Is that right? Do you also have to work on Saturday? What are your boss and your co-workers saying about your success? Please tell me all about it!

Later that year, in a letter dated September 1ˢᵗ, Ernst provided a long list of technical terms in English and then supplied Liselotte with their German equivalents, adding *I'd be happy to write you about other technical terms. Please, let me know.*

Even when his boss wasn't unsatisfied with his progress, Ernst got testy when his plans didn't always work out right away.

June 24, 1948

Yesterday my new machine was finished. Unfortunately, I had a small problem, because a needle bearing burned through after just five minutes. I'm really irritated about that. Everything had been running so smoothly, and now this thing happened. And so I spent today making improvements, and I hope that everything will work well now. My boss isn't even angry about it, but still I could tear out my hair. Oh, well—I know that your encouraging thoughts are always with me, and with this support I'll hopefully be successful and soon finish constructing this massive machine. Everything's actually working, but it's just too complicated to be ready for sale after the first test run. So, please keep your fingers crossed that this struggle will soon be behind me.

October 5, 1948

At work there's always a lot to do, irritating problems and, as you say in English now and then, [in English] *"trouble."* [in German] *Just yesterday the chief engineer, assistant engineer, and I discussed a fairly convoluted problem. After talking about it for more than an hour—and at the end it was a fairly heated exchange—I convinced them to accept my position, and the only thing that all of that brought was the headache of actually implementing all it. But it's a lot of fun for me, especially when the pressure's on.*

Liselotte continued to support all of his endeavors.

June 30, 1948

How is everything going as you prepare your machine for the exhibition? I'm keeping my fingers crossed, hoping that you'll be successful once again.

What are your colleagues saying, now that you're building another machine for the exhibition? I suppose that some are getting envious or even nasty—is that right?...Are you still always working in the evening, or don't you have an extra project at the moment?...I really do understand the way you explained this extra activity very well, and so I can only admire the way you have so much will power and stamina for all of this. You're certainly tired and exhausted in the evening because of your time at work. How does your mother feel about the things you're doing in addition to your job?

Only rarely did Ernst go into much detail about the nature of his machines.

October 10, 1948

Yesterday I had to work for half of the day in the firm even though the other sections of the company are shut down on Saturday. But what I'm doing now is very urgent, because the workshop is already waiting for it. It's a special injection molding machine that we'll be using ourselves, and the way it's put together has to be completely overhauled. I have one other draftsman who's working with me. In the meantime my other machine was sent off to the exhibition, and I'm eager to find out what the general public will say about it when it's introduced at the end of the month.

My firm got a letter from Germany...

At Super Mold Ernst was regularly able to combine work with pleasure with the help of some music from his homeland, something that might account for the stamina that Liselotte had commented on.

April 4, 1948

But now to something else. Twice each week the radio station in Lodi offers fifteen minutes' worth of Alpine melodies. During that time I'm an avid listener. In addition, these are often very well-known Ländler [a type of folk dance], polkas, and yodeling songs. While I'm listening, I treat myself to a glass of beer; this is my new sport. It's too bad that I don't have a beer stein from Munich here. I imagine that, when you read these words, you might even say: "This music has really gotten under Ernst's skin." If that's true, then I have to say that you're right. This treat happens every Wednesday and Friday between 12:30 and 12:45—and that's during my lunch break. At one o'clock I'm standing at my drafting table once again—sometimes, just like my colleagues, chewing on an eraser. Around 2:30 my boss usually comes in and says, [in English] *"Ernst, let's have a Coke"* [in German]. *I take him up on his invitation and then drink a Coca-Cola (which is definitely not a "Munich" type of beverage).*

His bilingual skills also proved to be helpful for his company.

April 26, 1948

A few weeks ago you proudly told me about the first time that you were able to put your knowledge of English to practical use. I'm glad that you enjoyed it. But can you imagine what happened to me today? Actually, it was something that was even better. My firm got a letter from Germany; all of it was written in German, and our business department couldn't handle it. And so the engineering section had to step in and help. I can't even describe how much fun I had with this. It had been two years since I'd read a business letter written in German. Translating it into English wasn't a problem at all, and our sales people were amazed at the way that I could magically decipher the job offer.

Since Liselotte was learning foreign languages at her evening classes, Ernst sometimes wrote her more extensively in English—for example, in this all-English section of a letter dated December 30, 1947:

Here in Lodi it's now wintertime as well. But as I've already told you, we haven't gotten any snow. I'm still working in the same plant…I'm glad my English is somewhat better now than it was when I came to America. But I'm still having lots of trouble, and I'm afraid that I'll never get away from my German accent. Twice a week I go to night school and study business English. I like this a lot.

While Liselotte devoted herself to learning languages, especially English, to open up better career opportunities, Ernst strove to become a member of the ASME—the American Society of Mechanical Engineers. To accomplish this he had to enlist the aid of his former employers in Munich, Therese Reiner and Doctor Gademan, and he asked Liselotte to help him out by acting as his intermediary.

September 1, 1948

It looks as if I'm giving Miss Reiner a lot of work to do. You've also been made aware of the situation. In my next letter I'll go into more detail about this, and I also hope to hear from you regarding this matter.

September 3, 1948

Please be so kind and let me know about the ASME business, if possible. How does Miss Reiner feel about it? I'm sorry if I'm burdening her with work, but I need to provide evidence about the work experience I've had up to now. You, my dear Liselotte, are the technical translator in this matter, and so I'll already thank you as well as Miss Reiner in advance for all of your efforts.

After Liselotte's intercession Frau Reiner immediately agreed to support Ernst's efforts.

September 9, 1948

And so I'm happy that Miss Reiner is helping me in connection with the ASME. The membership in this organization would definitely be a further step in my professional career. At the moment I only expect to become a junior member, because the requirements are very high and even my boss doesn't have a higher rank than this. However, if you don't belong to this organization, then your chances of getting ahead in this field in the U.S.A. are severely limited, because ASME engineers get more respect and preferential treatment everywhere. What do Miss Reiner and Doctor Gademan say about this? Please write me about it in more detail.

His goal wasn't an easy one to achieve. In a letter dated October 5, 1948, he fretted:

I haven't heard anything yet from the ASME, but I'm waiting for their letter every day, as well as news from Miss Reiner.

In a separate mailing, apparently sent later on that month, he continued to lament about the ASME's reticence.

I haven't heard anything yet from the professional organization, and I can't imagine why not. It's definitely a good thing that you're keeping your fingers crossed.

In his letter dated October 20, 1948, he went on in the same vein.

Miss Reiner's letter also arrived here a few days ago, but I still don't have an answer from New York about this matter. Who knows? Maybe everything has already failed. But I'll keep on waiting impatiently.

I wanted to become an electrical engineer ever since I was six years old...

The absence of news from the ASME was disheartening for him. In Germany his status as a half-Jew had prevented him from pursuing the advanced education that he'd yearned for, and now he felt it might be too late to make up for that disadvantage.

November 28, 1948

Right now I'm hitting the books on my own, learning about the theory of heat and steam generation. Up to now I haven't ever encountered a problem that I had to entrust to colleagues. It's actually the other way around—a lot of the time they come to me, hoping that I can dig up a formula in my German books and transpose it into American measurements...I really like my work at lot, but there are so many things in the world of machines that I don't understand at all, and unfortunately I'll also never have the chance to acquire such advanced knowledge—although it's definitely not that I don't want to learn. You know, when I look back on my life, then it really hurts. I wanted to become an electrical engineer ever since I was six years old, but—aside from all material or financial difficulties—such an advanced course of study was denied to me...The Reiner firm really helped me in all sorts of ways, and because of that I could go to night school, and I must honestly say that I've made use of every chance to learn. Often people ask me at work how I mastered all of this, and then I just have to think about the many hours that I've devoted to learning. I even completed assignments during the lunch break when I was an apprentice. I still had the faith that I'd be able to study at a university, but before I fully grasped what I was learning I had to use what I'd already absorbed up to that point to earn money.

I don't know myself why I'm writing all of this to you, but, you know, when I see the many students here who are as old as I am and are just starting to think about a career, who are merrily going to school and getting a diploma without a problem, then I always get depressed. My boss thinks that my practical experience makes me far superior to these students, but... The "but" means that such engineers attended an accredited school, and you need this to make a name for yourself, whereas I've just been working hard, and my progress in my career is more or less limited to good luck. The last point is most likely the reason for the unpleasantness with the ASME. I no longer have doubts that this will end in failure; the DAF course that I took probably won't be recognized, because it doesn't allow for direct verification. But because of my experiences in Germany I'm used to being shut out, and so in this case I can accept this type of treatment.

Now I've shared some of my melancholy thoughts with you, but don't worry about it; everything will still go well. Facts just can't be altered, and I won't try to prettify the facts about my past. But there are just so many things that I don't speak about with anyone, and so I ask that you understand when I tell you about them now and then. In all cases I'll definitely do everything that I can to get a higher position than just "junior engineer" before I pursue the plans I have regarding you. And a lot is hanging on that—don't you think?

The ASME bureaucracy continued to take its time.

January 15, 1949

I did, in fact, get news from the <u>ASME: unfortunately, they haven't yet reached a decision.</u>

Liselotte apparently underlined these words in Ernst's letter later on.

According to the letter, this organization is still waiting for Miss Reiner's information. I don't think that her letter was lost in the mail, but rather that the ASME doesn't consider Doctor Gademann to be the reference that I mentioned, because it's not supposed to be the confirmation of work in a firm, and so it seems logical that they're still waiting for Miss Reiner's answer. Therefore I've asked Miss Reiner to clarify this in a letter. Now I just hope that she'll help me out once again and maybe even put together a letter of recommendation for me. What do you think about this?

And then, abruptly, he sensed that his application was actually being considered.

January 27, 1949

Things are now apparently happening with my ASME application. Last week I had two telephone conversations about this matter from two very prominent engineers in San Francisco who are helping with this. In the meantime I hope that Miss Reiner has gotten my letter and that she fulfills my request; then things might still work out.

Liselotte was heartened to find out about the apparent progress.

February 2, 1949

First of all, though, about the ASME situation. Well, according to what you wrote the whole thing is now in motion once again. I also firmly believe that it will soon be successful, because Miss Reiner's letter will reach the organization during this time. I'd be so happy for you when that's finally a done deal, when it's finally settled.

News, when it did arrive early in the coming year, was discouraging.

February 26, 1949

By the way, I did get news from the ASME; I don't qualify in their eyes; I haven't learned enough to become a member. All the time that I was waiting I told you about it and hoped that it would all go smoothly so that

I might be worthier in your eyes. But this way it's like they say in Munich: I've failed to get the official recognition as an engineer. Please do me a favor: please don't mention anything about this in your letters, not even words of comfort. I don't want to deal with this anymore.

Although some details are lacking in the documents that survived, Ernst finally did realize his dream of ASME membership in 1951. Not only did he get into the organization and maintain his membership, he also served as vice chairman of the organization's Sacramento sub-section from 1958 to 1959.

He went on to get professional certification in 1967, when he passed the California State Board EIT (Engineer-in-Training) Test and, subsequently, the P.E. Examination in 1970. He became a Registered Mechanical Engineer, License No. 14911. The certificate bearing witness to his registration as a professional engineer is dated October 5, 1970.

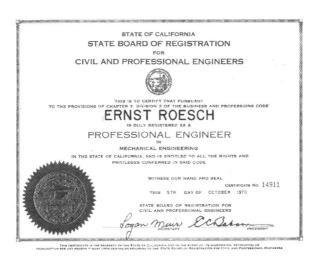

By 1980 he'd racked up ten U.S. patents for tire retreading machinery as well as corresponding foreign patents. In addition, in connection with his later work at Aerojet, he'd written or helped to write seven industry reports on aerospace technology—specifically, about turbomachinery development programs.

He wasn't able to achieve this solely through self-study, of course. Between 1959 and the end of 1963 he also completed a series of University of California extension courses in subjects such as "Oral Technical Communication," "Mechanics and Strength of Materials," and "Technical Writing and Expression."

This episode—Ernst's quest to qualify for ASME membership— illuminated an aspect of his life that I hadn't been privy to before. When we were all growing up, it was just a given that our father worked as an engineer and had the qualifications to do his job. Going through these particular letters gave me a new appreciation for his perseverance and drive, and especially his capacity to absorb so much complex scientific and mathematical information, to a large extent on his own.

His determination to achieve goals had a downside, though. He often seemed to believe that all problems could be solved and overcome through dedication, concentration, and the sheer application of will power—whether the issue was a technical one that came across his desk at Super Mold or Aerojet or an interpersonal one. When the problem he faced had something to do with raising us the way he saw fit or overcoming a difficult phase in his marriage, he approached it with the same type of resolve and focus, a strategy that wasn't always appropriate or effective. In matters of personal relationships, I came to feel, his conviction that all problems and difficulties had a neat solution, one that could be located and implemented, came to be a detriment and sometimes caused a lot of stress and unhappiness to fester inside him.

Lodi, California
December 30, 1947.

Dear Liselotte!

Today I want to write you again. How you see I am writing in English because you wanted me to a time ago. How are you? I hope you don't learn to hard and take it easy in your job, too. Have you been in the theatre lately? I hope you don't mind when I ask so many questions, but I am very much interested in how you are and in what's going on in my hometown.

Here in Lodi it is now wintertime, too. But as I have already told you, we haven't any snow. I am still working in the same plant. I have really got a good job and like my work very much. I am glad my English is somewhat better now than it was when I came to America. But I am still having lots of trouble, and I am afraid that I shall never get away from my German accent. Twice a week I go to night school and study business English. I like this very much.

Now to the main thing: "Happy Birthday"

CHAPTER FIVE

Education

The school is very strict and demanding.

When we were children, our parents always emphasized the importance of education—formal learning in a classroom as well as a broader openness to new facts and insights. I remember watching the likes of William Buckley's *Firing Line* and *Masterpiece Theater* regularly with both of them and having animated discussions with them afterwards. Once my mother and I watched two episodes of the 1970s British version of Tolstoy's *War and Peace* back to back—three hours in total—and never feeling bored or distracted for an instant.

Their attitudes reflected deep-rooted habits that they'd acquired and cultivated for many decades by that time, habits that they wanted to pass on to us. Both of them subscribed to the German notion of *Bildung*—something that's usually translated as "education," but a word that packs a much larger punch than just that. For many Germans like my parents, learning was something that involved self-improvement in an intellectual and also a moral and even a spiritual sense. This process was a lifelong enterprise, and it led you to see the world differently, more deeply, and to appreciate its complexity and its wonders.

Just like listening to concert music and marveling at nature, mastering new information and new skills helped both of them to cope with the harsh challenges that they'd encountered earlier in their lives. In his novel *The Once and Future King* T. H. White lets Merlin observe that

> [t]he best thing for being sad...is to learn something. That's the only thing that never fails. You may grow old and trembling in your anatomies, you may lie awake at night listening to the disorder of your veins, you may miss your only love, you may see the world about you devastated by evil lunatics, or know your honour trampled in the sewers of baser minds. There is only one thing for it then—to learn...That is the only thing which the mind can never exhaust, never alienate, never be tortured by, never fear or distrust, and never dream of regretting...

I'm not sure if they were familiar with White's book—though it wouldn't surprise me if both of them were—but the essence of Merlin's sentiments informed their lives. Learning for both of them was far more than merely a practical necessity for finding and holding on to decent employment.

Ernst, for example, was eager to hone his English language skills after he settled in Lodi.

November 4, 1947

Right now I'm going to evening classes and learning business English. You know, it's not that easy for an immigrant. But, when all is said and done, I need to try to learn the language in America as well as I can. I'm able to manage to a certain degree, but sometimes I don't know what to say, and then I have to wait until I can think of the right word. Of course, that's embarrassing. The biggest challenge is pronunciation; I always betray my origins as soon as I open my mouth. Americans are very helpful, and they don't make fun of you right away.

Liselotte took courses in English and Spanish, and she also learned how to drive.

October 19, 1946

Since this summer I've been going to language school, for the time being just to learn English. The school's very strict and demanding. But I still really hope that I'll be able to use the language one day. Exactly how, I don't know yet, but maybe my wish will be granted. I've always wanted to be a travel secretary or something like that, so that I can get away from here. But, please—don't tell anyone else about this; otherwise, if someone finds out about it, the others would think that I'm not very sensible. I also wrote the exam for my driver's license on June 18th, 1946, and so now I can finally drive a car myself. Unfortunately, I hardly ever have the chance to do it…The test wasn't easy at all. The actual driving wasn't that bad for me, but I almost thought that I'd failed the theoretical exam. I spent eight to twelve o'clock in the police testing center, and I came out at one o'clock with the driver's license in my hand—beaming with happiness.

Not surprisingly, given his hopes for their future, Ernst encouraged her to pursue one subject in particular.

April 12, 1947

You write that you're diligently learning languages. I personally wish that you could especially use the English language in the future. What do you think about that?

He also did his part to facilitate her progress. In April 1947, after he sent off a shipment her way, he let her know that *I put newspapers into your package because of your interest in the English language.*

Liselotte took advantage of all the reading material that he'd provided. When he told her that he was shipping even more to her, she responded on June 11, 1947.

I already wrote to you that I've stopped learning Spanish for the time being. You know, <u>Life</u> is a very interesting magazine. It gives me a lot to read until I'm done with the whole thing. The other one, the one with the songs, is also very nice. The German ones are the most interesting; you can understand the German texts in a totally different way. When I read them, I can really see the way life looks and feels where you are.

The relative dearth of periodicals in Germany made her especially grateful for Ernst's help.

I'm also already looking forward to the newspapers, because you can especially learn a lot by reading. Are these magazines? They're a lot easier to read. Here there are some to buy now and then, but you have to be lucky to get your hands on some.

Later on he showed his willingness to guide her through the labyrinth of English expressions.

October 20, 1948

However, in case you have some questions about English colloquialisms, I'd be happy to help you. You asked me if I had a technical dictionary. Yes—you gave me a dictionary like that for my twenty-first birthday, remember? By the way, it's done yeoman's service for me. Actually, I'm familiar with many technical terms in English but not in German, because I didn't use these words in Germany. But still I definitely know ten times as many technical terms in German than in English.

Liselotte's schedule, a full-time job as well as night courses, was a demanding one, and it began to take its toll on her.

April 28, 1947

In my last letter I told you that I'm learning so much when I'm not at work. Just imagine: during the past few weeks I've always been so dizzy whenever I walk even a short distance; last week I went to the doctor, and he diagnosed a general weakness, and so now I've given up all of my courses for the time being, except for English. Of course, my condition hasn't gotten all that bad, but still my health is more important than these classes. I've now gotten pills to swallow; I really hope that they'll help me a little.

When Ernst nonetheless expressed concern about her health, she sought to assuage his anxieties.

June 26, 1947

I'm really sorry that I wrote all of that business about swallowing pills, etc., because it's really not as bad as you now imagine it is. Please, don't get upset about it. I'm still going to the language school because I can't just quit so easily and, besides, I've already stopped attending the other language lessons. And so I'm asking you once again not to get upset about that. And, you know, whether I really need the languages or not, you can always use the skills that you have, and it's also something pleasant.

She decided to keep on attending her English class despite the risks to her safety that her decision entailed.

August 20, 1947

You can think about me on the first of September—that's when the English course starts again. It takes place every Monday and Thursday from six o'clock to seven-thirty, but now it already gets dark again at that time, and I'm not exactly scared, but I'm also not completely comfortable with this situation, either. But, you know, I also considered taking a break from the course for a while, but then you forget a lot, because when I'm at home—and also when I don't go to class—I'm not learning anything.

Exams in the course proved to be demanding.

December 13, 1947

Please think about me on January 27, 1948, and keep your fingers crossed for me. That's when I'll take my big English test from six to eight o'clock. Eight people in our class weren't even allowed to take the examination. I did get permission to write the exam, but it's extraordinarily difficult. You know, there are a lot of questions that test my knowledge and also political terms that I don't know how to say in German. I have five minutes to translate each question and answer it. Please keep your fingers crossed.

A sizable majority of the participants dropped out at the end of the first term. Early in 1948 Liselotte wrote:

Today in English it was the end of the semester. We'll start class once again on May 10, 1948. Seven of the fifty original students will continue; the course has been too demanding for the others. Sometimes it's really very strenuous to have this intellectual stress after a day at work.

The pace of her schedule, coupled with the harshness of a Bavarian winter, kept affecting her health.

January 22, 1948

My English test was yesterday…Right now I have a pretty bad cold, and just yesterday I could hardly speak. The change in the weather causes that; it's gotten colder again. Besides that I've had awful headaches and pains in my throat—everything happening just when my test took place. But I still took the risk and wrote the exam. It was tough, as I'd expected, and of course I don't know yet whether I passed or not. I'll find out about that on January 28th or 29th. That's soon enough. I'll tell you exactly what my score was. There were five questions—not very short ones. I needed to answer them, translate them, and mostly provide reasons for my answers to most of them (my personal opinion). You probably think that I'm exaggerating, but it wasn't that easy. After the exam we had to complete a lengthy dictation that dealt with—according to what I understood, anyway—the struggles and tribulations of the inhabitants [in English] *"of the Outer Hebrides."* [in German] *And I'll end my letter on that note; otherwise it might get boring for you. The class lasted from six o'clock to 7:45 PM.*

Given the realities of post-war Germany—the presence of British and American occupation forces, for example—it's not surprising that her teacher's curriculum included both British and American English.

February 7, 1948

My evening school class is now in full swing again. It's really nice! I have an instructor who wants to teach us British as well as American pronunciation.

We also have very difficult translations, and sometimes we have to translate right away, orally, without having much time to think things over. Most of the time in class is devoted to activities like these. But I think that I can learn a lot from him. On the first day of the course I found a seat in the front row so that I can understand and hear everything. When I've completed this level, then I'll also learn English shorthand.

In spite of the tough challenges Liselotte kept making swift progress.

February 27, 1948

Thanks for asking me about how I'm doing. I'm doing well, and I know you are, too! My English exam went well…Now we're back to learning. Are you also taking courses again, or don't you have enough students for a new class?

Ernst was happy to hear about her test results.

March 8, 1948

But now to the main point of my letter: [in English, including Ernst's spelling error] *"My congratulation."* [in German] *I never had the slightest doubts about your test. How long do you still have to go to school until you can write the final exam? Are you planning to take a translator exam? I admire your immense interest in languages. For me, English is more or less just a necessary evil. But, when you speak it every day, then it becomes something of a habit so that the English words mostly occur to you faster than the German ones. Even when I sometimes meet with Germans, I speak in English. Still, it'll take a long time until I've truly mastered the English language, especially the way difficult words are used. I especially need a lot more practice when it comes to writing. But I should really apply myself to learn it well. Maybe someday I can make use of it as a technical translator. (This is, of course, just a dream.)*

Liselotte's zest for learning English never waned, in stark contrast to the attitude of many of her classmates.

March 9, 1948

My English class is also very interesting. There are supposed to be fifty students in the class, and about twenty of us are still there. Only a small minority is able to keep up. Mostly people just don't have the stamina. It's very demanding when you go home after work, and it's still cold or rainy on top of everything else, and then you have to go to school after that. But I'm doing this more because it gives me pleasure and because I enjoy it.

Just like Ernst, Liselotte continued to consider getting a translating credential.

March 18, 1948

Thanks for [in English, including Liselotte's misspelling] *your congratulation!* [in German] *It really wasn't a sure thing with that examination of mine. I didn't have much hope because so many questions had to do with political topics. I was just lucky when it came to this test! I don't even know when our final exam will be because I think it'll still be two to three years from now if it all works out—if I don't flunk a few times before then. But then I'll also have the translator examination—but will I be able to pass that one? I think that you're already able to speak very well in English. That's what I can't do. I don't have enough access to English speakers—I mean, to practice speaking. I do get enough practice in writing English. You shared your thoughts about becoming a technical translator. It'd be good if you could reach that goal!!*

A new instructor arrived who had unusually high expectations for his English students, but Liselotte seemed to appreciate his more rigorous standards. She shared some of his instructional methods in a letter hailing from May 1948:

My English course started up again on Monday. We have a new teacher. He's a very large man! The translation from German into English that we have to complete for tomorrow deals with this topic—"instructions for a washing machine with two containers"—and we also have to fluently retell a story (narrated in English) that he only told us once in English; and we have to turn in our rewritten, corrected dictation, in addition to various other smaller tasks. The last time when he told us a short story in English, I had to laugh about it—and so then I was the one who had to retell it in English right away. He's really very tough, this guy, but we're learning quite a lot!

She maintained a packed program over the next few years. In her letter dated September 22, 1948, she told Ernst:

Today I'm writing with the typewriter again; this just goes faster. I still have to cook something and help out in the kitchen, and after that it'd be too late to write to you. In the last few days we've been putting in overtime at work until seven o'clock; after that I had to go to school once, and I got back home at around eight thirty. That's an awfully long day. Unfortunately life isn't that nice here where we are, and it's not made easy for us.

A letter postmarked January 9, 1949, showed her still seeking to boost her English skills.

I have to write another English exam this Tuesday. At first I didn't even want to do it, but Miss Reiner thinks that I should take a stab at it. But I never believe that I'll be able to pass. They're always so demanding; maybe I won't even turn in my test.

Ernst's ability to speak English clearly impressed her.

September 30, 1948

You must already be able to talk in English very well, because leading a discussion like that for an entire hour would mean getting your language certificate right away. Well, of course, you'd also have to complete writing and translating tasks, but still the ability to speak is a big plus. Here only the young American women can speak fluently in German; the others just babble or beat around the bush.

During the same time Ernst took pains to hone his grasp of formal English. On October 17, 1948, at eleven in the evening, he set aside his work at his drawing board at home and wrote to Liselotte.

I also have to prepare an English assignment, because right now I'm taking private lessons again so that I can learn to distinguish between formal English and my slang, which resembles Bavarian German and makes me stand out from the natives.

And now I'd like to ask you for a small favor, dear Liselotte...

Facility with American English was hardly enough for Ernst, however. To make progress in his profession he needed to study and master advanced material in his field, and he enlisted Liselotte's assistance in locating some key German books for him, texts that were easier for him to absorb than technical works in English. He was eager to get copies of them—in particular the Dubbel reference works—and Liselotte was willing to help him out

January 30, 1948

And now I'd like to ask you for a small favor, dear Liselotte, but only if it's possible for you to do this. Do you have access to technical books? It'd be a great help for me if I owned the Dubbel machine handbook (two volumes) or Harder's Guides for Machine Construction *(three volumes). Over here I can't get my hands on them. I've already looked everywhere I could think of. Maybe you could be so kind and check around for me. These don't have to be new books, but please only do this if it's not a problem for you. I'd be happy to pay you back for your expenses as soon as it's possible to send money to you.*

Liselotte took this undertaking seriously and devoted a lot of time and effort to tracking down everything Ernst mentioned. Her efforts gradually paid off, which earned his heartfelt gratitude.

March 2, 1948

Well, today I was really speechless. Now I'm even getting packages from you. I couldn't believe my eyes, [in English] *but there it was,* [in German] *a package from Germany, and on top of that something from Liselotte. Before I even thought about opening it up, I checked it out from all angles, and only then did I look at what was inside. All right, I really have to say that you've really put together a wonderful surprise. A technical dictionary. On top of that I also found a wonderfully colored card, and it became clear that this was a birthday present for me. Then I was twice as happy right away; this time around, when it came to the mail, fortune smiled on me. I have to consider how I can repay you for this. I thank you from the very bottom of my heart. But, my dear friend, you shouldn't put yourself into so much debt, not to mention the amount you paid for shipping. (I could tell how much it cost from the markings.) Well, my deepest thanks to you once more. I hope that it's all right with you if I use the lovely technical dictionary even before my birthday comes around. As a matter of fact, I can really put it to good use.* [in English] *Is it O.K. when I use it right away?*

Not all of the items on Ernst's wish list were as easy to hunt down, though, as Liselotte let him know on March 9, 1948.

You know, so far I haven't been able to get your books. It's incredibly difficult, but please don't be distraught. I still think that I'll be able to do this for you. I'll keep trying to get this done if it's a way to help you out a little.

March 18, 1948

I haven't found out anything about your books yet. You know, it looks as if I still have a chance to get them at one place, though I'm not sure if I'll succeed. However, I still haven't gotten a definite "No." I really hope that I'll still be able to buy them. Besides that, a man in a bookstore promised that I should be able to get the Dubbel during the summer, when the new books arrive. Maybe I'll hit the jackpot then!

Failure wasn't an option for her.

May 16, 1948

Unfortunately, I haven't gotten your books yet. I'm really sorry about that, but it hasn't been possible to locate them yet. I definitely won't forget about it, dear Ernst. You can depend on that!

Probably because of tenacity she exhibited, Ernst felt emboldened to ask her to track down even more titles.

August 1, 1948

Now, my dear Liselotte, I have to tell you about something else that's painful for me. I've wanted to do this for a long time, but I felt awkward about it. Actually I shouldn't do it, because I know that at the moment you definitely don't have the money for this. And so I ask you not to be angry with me, and if it's not possible, then just don't do it. You know that at one time many books were burned, and before I traveled to America I could hardly get replacements for them. Because of that I don't have any German reference books here at all when it comes to one subject. All I've got is books in English. Maybe it's now possible to get the same book that I used to have in Germany. Its title is <u>Mathematik der Maxima, Minima und Optima</u>, *and it's written by Dr. Ing. [Doctor of Engineering] W. Ortlepp; it was published by the Carl Creutzburg Publishing House in Dresden. But please do this only if you're okay with it and if you can handle this financially. I've made some inquiries, and it's still impossible to send money to Germany. Please, please, my dear Liselotte, don't be angry with me, because if it's not at all possible, then it doesn't really matter.*

Later on, recognizing that her search might not succeed, Ernst sought to assuage her.

September 20, 1948

My dear Liselotte, regarding the books I want to let you know that I have a "Klingelnberg"—that's what you meant with the word "Klingenfeld." It's a very good book, but it's limited to machine tools and operating techniques, whereas as far as I know the Dubbel volumes deal with machine construction in general—that is, also with hydraulics, pumps, steam generators, etc.—and I especially need reference material for that last category. But if you just can't get them, don't exert yourself any further. I know you mean well, and I know that it wouldn't be your fault. Please understand me the right way, my darling.

Liselotte persevered.

October 3, 1948

In connection with your Dubbel I pulled every possible string yesterday. I was angry when I was told that a copy had come in, but that I wasn't able to get that one. That's why I had a very serious conversation with this man and got him to promise that he'll send me a card right away if another copy *comes into his store. If he says this, he'll definitely be true to his word. This is someone who's already helped me out many times when I was in a bind. For example, last year at Christmas I didn't have anything special for Miss Reiner. It's always so difficult to find a gift for her. Then, even though there didn't seem to be any books, I still got something. He's also already ordered your book <u>Maxima Optima</u>… from the publisher, but so far he hasn't received a response. They don't carry it in their bookstore. So, once again, we have a chance of getting this book, and I hope that it works out. I'd really be so glad if I could help you out a little.*

Later that year she sent him another package.

October 9, 1948

I've finally gotten some technical books today. Unfortunately I wasn't able to get the three-volume Dubbel anywhere. I can say that I was in almost every bookstore that could possibly have carried it. Here we only have the short version of the Dubbel, which is what I'm sending to you. I was also only able to get these two used volumes of Harder—I was very lucky to find them. If the third volume comes to the bookstore again, then it'll be set aside for me. I just hope that all of this is at least a small help for your work as you construct your machines. Beyond that, I ordered the book <u>Maxima</u> quite a while ago, but so far I haven't been able to get it. I hope that all of this gets to you in good condition. When I imagine the journey that these need to complete before they arrive at your house! I send you many dear greetings and am, as always, just your supportive Liselotte.

Christmas came early for Ernst in 1948 when Liselotte's books showed up.

November 10, 1948

Above all I want to thank you so much for the package of books that just reached me in the meantime. I was immensely happy to get it, and I have to wonder how you were able to get your hands on all of these volumes. I'm just afraid that you had to spend a lot of money for them. The books really contain very valuable information, and the small book by Dubbel is especially very helpful, despite its size. The Harder is also very good, of course, but the Dubbel is really a flawless compilation of formulas, etc.

Later that month, in a separate letter dated November 25, 1948, he let her know again that *"The Dubbel material is especially fantastic."*

In the following year Liselotte kept acting as his guardian angel when it came to the technical material he needed. In a letter postmarked January 9, 1949, she wrote:

Today I ordered your technical newspaper. It comes out once every month, and it's sent to me. When I get a copy, then I'll send it on to you. It's called "Workshop and Workplace," and it has illustrations and explanations. I don't understand any of it; please write me at some point and let me know if it's worthwhile for you. For the time being there are only two. The other one, though, is a monthly publication that an organization puts out. It's pointless to send you that one. You don't have to send me an American newspaper; that wouldn't be money well spent. I can buy some of those here, and I do buy some now and then.

When Liselotte was growing up in Munich, a whole spectrum of topics fascinated and intrigued her—science, foreign languages like Spanish and Russian, the world of the theater, and the universe of books. At one point her parents thought about sending her to an academy for girls, and they seriously pursued this possibility for a while. As our mother told us much later, though, they were told that she couldn't be admitted into the school, given that, according to the pseudoscientific biases of the time, her ears were "too big."

As her correspondence with my father made clear, however, this was hardly the only hardship that she faced early on.

Meine liebe Liselotte!

Ich kann es nicht unterlassen, dir heute noch einige Zeilen zu schreiben. Den ganzen Abend denke ich unentwegt an dich und versuche mir vorzustellen, wie du wohl dieses Fest verbringst. Meine Mutter ist bereits zu Bett gegangen, aber ich sitze immer noch beim Lichtschein des Christbaumes. Inmitten meiner Geschenke, welche ich von meiner Mutter erhielt, steht dein Bild, welches ich bereits eingerahmt habe, und deine so schöne Weihnachtskarte. Du hättest mir wirklich keine größere Freude machen können. Ich weiß nicht ob es dir auch so geht, aber ich denke Weihnachten's immer über die verflossenen Weihnachtsfeste nach. Wenn ich aber gerade dein Bild ansehe, dann träume schon von den kommenden. Du hast mir zwar geschrieben ich sollte keine Pläne schmieden, aber ...... Als ich heute vormittag noch im Geschäft arbeitete, dachte ich immer daran, daß doch in meiner Heimat schon Weihnachtsabend ist. Meine Gedanken waren bestimmt nicht am Ladentisch sondern in München und wie ich so an dich dachte, wollte ich

CHAPTER SIX

Hardships

I'm writing the first part of this letter by candlelight...

Even after I'd gotten a deeper sense of the grave difficulties and challenges that both of my parents faced during their childhood and youth in Nazi Germany, I naively thought that the conclusion of the war put an end to their troubles and that they had a far better life when it was over. Many anecdotes in their correspondence taught me otherwise, though. When it came to lighting, safety, and even basic necessities like food, the years following VE Day proved to be anything but easy.

An array of hardships confronted Liselotte after the war ended. As I already mentioned earlier on, for example, the classroom where she learned English in 1947 had no heat. Its windows had no glass, only cardboard.

Locating a decent place to live proved to be difficult for her, as well as finding basic consumer goods like shoes.

October 19, 1946

It took three weeks for me to get your birthday letter because my address had changed. In any case I want to thank you a lot for the nice surprise. At that time I was really impressed that you could send me that! Just at that time my parents had, in fact, found a property to renovate and enlarge on Infanterie Street. It's actually a barracks, but it's a practical location for the workshop and the storage area. It's not a particularly good place to live in. But, my God, you really have to be happy about it. When it comes to living quarters, there's still some scarcity here. Actually nothing much has changed since you left—I mean in terms of our living conditions...I could only get a single pair of shoes so far. Of course, you know about this business yourself. I hope that something might change soon.

Toward the end of the same letter Liselotte noted that Therese Reiner continued to act as a fairy godmother of sorts for her, as she did for us children later on. After a bomb hit her family's house during an air raid, she was able to find accommodations in Frau Reiner's home.

Much of Munich had been destroyed in the course of the war, and reconstruction was a long and arduous process, as Liselotte remarked in her letter dated April 28, 1947.

Actually, there aren't any new things to report from Munich. Progress is being made very slowly; it's also clear that, before anything else, the rubble needs to be removed. The office building on the Fahn Street is also being built again. As far as I know, the construction has already progressed quite a bit, but still there's a shortage of various building materials.

All in all, conditions have become terrible during the last few months.

Postwar Munich also suffered from an absence of regular, reliable electricity, something that Liselotte bemoaned now and then.

October 5, 1947

During the night there's already frost, and during the day it's dry. But we desperately need rain. In the evening hours during the week (eight to nine-thirty) we don't have any light; that's really very terrible. Hopefully it'll be better again during the winter.

In the same letter she noted:

Now, above all, it's already pitch-black when I walk back home from school. I still have to get used to that.

On the other hand, she refrained from attending plays for a while.

October 24, 1947

Now the time for going to the theater is pretty much over, because you can't walk on the streets safely anymore when it's dark. Here we now have so many foreigners; all of them are so mean, and even during the daytime they often mug the Germans. In such conditions, going out would be too risky. Yesterday I didn't even go to school, because walking home is a little discomforting. But now I'll go to school again; that was just an exception!

Imagine—I wrote the first part of this letter by candlelight, because it's only later on that we'll get light again, and it was already so dark. That's actually quite romantic, don't you think?

Despite these conditions, Liselotte wrote in the same letter, she was trying to maintain a positive outlook.

You write that I never mention how things are really going in my life. Well, believe me, that's not so easy to answer, because I do write to you about the things I'm experiencing, etc.—and my everyday existence. I've already gotten smart enough to recognize that I'm fortunate if things stay the way that they are now. I mean that, given the circumstances here in this country, you shouldn't expect and hope for anything at all, but rather just live from day to day…But making plans or resolutions just isn't appropriate over here anymore, because instead of getting better things are always getting even worse. So, dear Ernst, please don't believe that things are going badly for me personally—no!…Please, don't worry about me, because this is something that we can't ever change.

At times Liselotte reported about labor unrest in the city, even though, as a nonunion worker, she wasn't directly involved in these work actions.

January 22, 1948

Something very unusual is happening today around here. Just imagine— people are refusing to work for twenty-four hours. And the streetcars are affected, starting at midnight and going on until midnight tomorrow. But I'm not "organized." Tomorrow I'll go to work, of course, but I'm curious to see how things are. You know, they want to give us—or, more to the point, they're giving us—seventy-five grams of fat during this period, and in the next period it'll most likely be no fat at all. All in all, conditions have become terrible during the last few months. In general people are very pessimistic here. I also don't know what to believe. I don't always believe what I hear. A lot of it is just empty talk.

When it came to the economic circumstances around her, she saw no signs of improvement whatsoever.

April 7, 1948

I've heard that as of May we'll be able to send air mail letters to America; I still don't know for sure, and I don't know whether this will only be possible for business letters. This information hasn't been made public yet. Thanks for asking—I'm doing the same as always—I can say that I'm doing well. Here where we are the living conditions that most people must contend with are impossible, and there's no sign that things will improve! Is everything still so expensive where you are? Are groceries getting even more expensive? A short time ago I heard a debate about this topic; it suggested that the living standard of thousands of American families has been jeopardized because of this. Easter was very nice here because we didn't have to work for four days. For once this was a longer amount of time!

Liselotte kept a stiff upper lip about the dire conditions surrounding her, or at least she characterized herself that way in a letter from June 1948.

Over here there are large hunger strikes. No streetcars have been in service for the entire week—since Saturday. At least you can go where you need to go on foot; no big deal, we can handle it! We're dealing with circumstances that you can't even imagine!

In a letter that probably also stemmed from June 1948 she added these sentiments.

Thank God, I'm always doing well, and personally I can't complain, even if circumstances are always getting worse where we are. You really can't imagine at all what things are like here, and real Americans couldn't grasp it at all—that there are things like this, and that people endure all of these things during the entire year. It's not getting better at all, not even a little bit better! I think that I'll have gray hair by the time conditions have changed!

In addition to economic misery there were ominous political storm clouds.

September 22, 1948

Today I'm writing with the typewriter again; this just goes faster. I still have to cook something and help out in the kitchen, and after that it'd be too late to write to you...

Today I read about different suggestions for the equalization of financial burdens. I'd have to pay three or four more taxes than I've been paying up to now. In that case, really, I'd just be working so that I could pay taxes. And as for the Berlin situation, I also don't know what will happen there. You can already assume, even if it sounds terrible, that there'll still be fighting there at some point. It's just bad for us because the Russians are already located so deep inside the country that if the entire conflict took place here, in Germany, we'd experience all sorts of terrible things again, and we already had to endure so much during the last war. We've already suffered from and had to deal with all these indescribably awful things. Please, Ernst, I'm sorry that I've now written all of this, but all day long you hear so much about such things that you find yourself focusing on them automatically, even if you don't want to. But for the time being I won't let myself be robbed of courage—and then, of course, things haven't gotten that far yet. Let's also hope that it all works out well.

If there's something that you really want, feel free to write to me...

Early on Ernst started helping Liselotte out with a series of care packages.

September 15, 1946

So what's new in my home town? Please write and tell me about everything. What sorts of things have you been up to? Are the food shortages still so severe in your area? In the next few days I'll send a small package to you. When it comes to food, there aren't any shortages here, and as much as possible I'm happy to support the people in Germany who are special to me with groceries.

He invited her to let him know which items he should locate and send her way.

April 12, 1947

As I see in your letter, it's not going that well with you, but you're just claiming to be content because there's nothing that can possibly be done. Here in America we don't have to worry about food, but we do have to worry about money, and except for those who are financially independent, that's true for everyone. Where you live, scarcity is everywhere, as I know from my own experience. If there's something that you really want, feel free to write to me, and as much as possible I'll help you with advice or with things that you need. Please don't hesitate.

Liselotte expressed her gratitude for his shipments as well as her guilt about not being to return the favor.

June 11, 1947

Yesterday I got a card notifying me that your package has arrived here. Of course, I took time off this morning and picked it up right away at the customs office. I really have to say that I was dumbfounded when I saw so many items, and above all the way that you packed everything up so nicely. Even the clerk at the post office said that this was a "sweet" package. But I was also extremely happy—and you can pretty much imagine this—that such a shipment was sent to me personally. Above all, you took great care to select all of these things, and they're all of such good quality. So accept my thanks from the bottom of my heart. Unfortunately, at the moment it's impossible for me to brighten your life by sending you something. But in spite of this I want to ask you not to send such packages all that often, because it surely costs you a lot of money, and I think that you really need your money to buy essential things for your mother and yourself. Your task—to provide for everything—is already a big one. Miss Reiner and Gisela were also very happy about your beautiful package. When I write this, I don't want to suggest that they were expecting me to share a lot of things with them, but that they were impressed with the way that you put the shipment together. I haven't told my parents yet about what you sent me. They'll only find out about it when I bring them something sweet to eat. Recently Daddy has been crazy about sweets. At work today, of course, I needed to tell people that I had to pick up my package from America. They were so mean and envious, and they felt that I needed to bring the package back to the office—I think they felt that I should share its contents with them. I brought back small samples for them; otherwise, I think, I wouldn't have been able to get back home safely. Gisela and Miss Reiner were completely outraged about the way that my colleagues and my boss behaved. The way people can just forget how to act! But this is just the way it is here nowadays. If one person gets something and others find out about it, then there's a huge amount of envy. But, you know, that won't upset me anymore. I've already forgotten about what happened today—the "friendly words," I mean.

Another package that Ernst sent—a *Christkindl,* or Christmas present—took an especially long time to get to its destination.

January 6, 1948

And so you've sent something to me once again! Of course, I'm curious to see what's in it, but I'm not in a position financially to give you any presents. This way I'm just in your debt, and it's a debt that I'm not able to pay off.

The package hasn't arrived yet, but I hope it's just been delayed. As soon as it gets here, I'll let you know.

One challenge that Liselotte faced now and then was how to mete out portions of Ernst's care packages to her co-workers.

July 23, 1947

I also wanted to let you know that I had something like a snack's worth of food from the contents the package, because once again I didn't share it the way that you imagined that I would. Each of my colleagues got just a small portion—definitely not more than that—because I didn't want to just choose a few people to get some.

You know, I always get red with embarrassment when I buy something like that.

One daunting task for Ernst, as things turned out, was locating the exact type of stockings that Liselotte had described to him in her letters. Just as she went all out to hunt down the books that he needed, he pulled out all the stops to get exactly what she wanted.

On November 10, 1948, he claimed that he'd sent another parcel, one to honor her on her Catholic name day, and done so less expeditiously so that he'd have more cash left over for the all-important stockings.

I only found out when your name day was very recently, and so I wanted to send at least a trifle to you via air mail. In the meantime your actual name day present is coming your way, but it's not going as an air mail parcel…Just imagine—it would have cost me $6.50, and I really didn't want to pay that much and fritter away that much money. And so I opted to send it with the regular mail service. Please understand this, my dear Liselotte, but it wasn't worth so much money to send this small item as air mail. Now I'm just annoyed that it'll get to you late. But look—with the amount I saved I can buy you three pairs of nylon stockings, and I think that's more practical, right?

He felt no small amount of anxiety about shipping off the wrong sort of product. When he put together his November 13, 1948 letter to Liselotte, he included a small picture in the envelope, part of a newspaper advertisement. The picture shows a woman's legs wearing stockings, and Ernst's words on the right side read, in English, *"Is that the thing you wanted?...If so, you are not going to get it."*

He elaborated on this point in his actual letter.

Dear Liselotte, you know that I'm willing to do everything that I possibly can for you. You are very, very modest and don't ask for much. However, when it comes to what you told me you wanted...I have to ask you a question. Do you really want "net" nylon stockings, as you've written? I just can't imagine that's the case, because I don't think that something like that could be considered modern where you are. Here only dancing girls wear those sorts of stockings.

Fortunately for him, Eddie Stritzel's wife could act as his trusty guide in the world of women's clothing.

Because I personally didn't trust my judgment, I looked for someone to advise me and decided to place my trust in Mrs. Stritzel. When I talked with her, I got an in-depth lesson in women's stockings. She filled me in on a special sort of nylon stocking which supposedly doesn't get runs, and it's different from the so-called fish net dancing-girl stockings. So, my dear Liselotte, what should I buy? Can you remember which [in English, and capitalized] *"American Trade Name"* [in German] *it is? Please, my darling, write me the exact details, and I'll definitely send exactly what you want, but if you want the type of stockings that are in the picture I've enclosed, I just don't understand that. Please don't be angry that I shared all of this with Mrs. Stritzel, but she's really understanding. By the way, she stood up for you and told me forcefully,* [in English] *"Whatever she wants, you are going to get it for her!"* [in German] *That's the exact command that she gave me.*

He was soon relieved to learn that Liselotte didn't have fishnet stockings in mind at all.

November 28, 1948

Once again I'm glad that you don't want any "dancing girl" stockings. I was right to think that something like that couldn't be true. I was beaming with happiness when I told Mrs. Stritzel about it, and meanwhile I asked her to get a pair of what I assumed were the right stockings when she could. You know, I always get red with embarrassment when I buy something like that. Just a short while ago when I asked for the newest color—you know, all of the questions—[in English] long or short, how thin, what gauge, size—[in German] and also with so many young women close by in the ladies' clothing section, etc.—Oh, my God, now I've put my foot in my mouth again, haven't I? But before you wonder what's going on, I'd better let you know that the stockings that I bought recently are meant for you and that they've already been en route to you for about six weeks now. Now I just really couldn't keep that to myself any longer.

Oh well, soon Christmas will be here, and I hope that all of it reaches you in good shape. Please let me know right away when it arrives.

The arrival of Ernst's package brought unexpected consequences. In one of her 1948 letters Liselotte told him about the way some of her co-workers had reacted.

Please, dear Ernst, I didn't mean it that way when it comes to the stockings—that you now think that you have to make up for something you neglected to do. No, no—I really don't want that. Even though it's so nice to actually have something special for once, I don't want you to go out of your way and spend money for me again. Of course, some people at work were agitated when I was wearing "American stockings." That's something that you can't even imagine. I didn't even know that these stockings were also in short supply in America. As far as reciprocity goes, we'll have to see, because if I can find something suitable for you again, then I'd naturally get it for you.

I wasn't even able to attend the funeral, and I'll never forgive myself for that.

In many ways Ernst met with good fortune during his early years in the States. He benefitted from an exciting job, from prospects of professional advancement, from the availability of educational opportunities, and from a small but supportive circle of friends, especially the Stritzels. On the other hand, as he made clear to Liselotte on occasion, he sometimes felt alienated and isolated in California, and he yearned for the familiar sights and sounds of his youth.

In this regard Liselotte also proved herself to be a true friend.

March 1, 1947

Up to this point I've been content. California is a wonderful place, and I could tell you a lot about it. But not everything can fit into a letter. My greatest joy comes from my work. Some of the massive machines that I've been constructing are already finished. Until now everything that "the man from Germany" made has worked all right. Three months ago I was promoted to junior engineer. A short while ago my boss told me that I'm his second-best engineer. No one else in my office speaks German, and so I need to speak in English all day long. I can already manage pretty well; it's just that sometimes my pronunciation makes it hard for the Americans to understand me. I'm very happy that I have the opportunity to work in my field. I can only speak German in the evenings with my mother. This is the reason why I'm not answering your letter in English. Besides, I'm already very homesick for Munich anyway. I often think about the few good friends that I had, the ones who stood by me. Do you still remember those uncertain times? In the darkroom you always gave me a reason to hope…But, in spite of the times, we spent some very wonderful hours together at work, didn't we?

Liselotte sensed how profound his discontent could be, and she sympathized with him as she had in the past.

October 24, 1947

You also write that you're content, but, you know, many times I think that you're still suffering from homesickness. Please excuse me if I remind you about something, but I think so often about how tough that is. I hope that I haven't done something stupid now by writing that! Please don't be angry with me because of this. I remember the time in the Reiner Company very well—especially all of the things you had to endure because of your mother, and your other concerns and problems. I still remember it all very clearly.

Her sympathetic words encouraged him to share more about what troubled him. The ugliness of some of the events in his past haunted him, for example, and the need to speak English almost all of the time—a language that wasn't his native tongue—also put him at odds with his surroundings.

December 3, 1947

But when you ask me about being homesick…then my answer is simple. When I live far away and speak another language every day, then I often have memories of Munich, my home town, and I hope to be able to see it once more. When I occasionally think about the times that I lived through in Munich, then I just hope and wish that humanity will become more intelligent at some point. But it'd be sheer stupidity to place all of the blame on my homeland, because this place has also seen better times.

Ernst's Christmas letter in 1948 revealed his occasional nostalgia and longing for the strains of his mother tongue.

December 25, 1948

Now I want to tell you a little about myself. Right after Christmas Eve I wrote to you and told you some things about it. I spent yesterday at home with my mother. Several people came by to visit, mostly people who speak German. What deeply affected me was a radio program with Christmas greetings from many different nations. Can you imagine how that is when you're listening to a shortwave program over here, hearing reports from soldiers in Wiesbaden and Christmas greetings from the airfield in Berlin? Even if it was all in English, it still meant a lot to me. If I just owned a shortwave radio, I thought, then there'd certainly also be a program in German. Maybe you can find out when German shortwave programs are broadcast, and on which wavelength. Then maybe I could visit people I know here and listen to programs like that with them.

An especially traumatic blow struck him late in 1947, something that forced him to recognize just how far away he was from Germany.

November 27, 1947

I've just gotten back from my evening walk, which I took so that I could think about a long list of things. As I hashed over so many memories, I had to think about you, because you know, at least roughly, about everything that's happened to me during the last few years. When I promised in my last letter to send you another one soon, I never would have thought that I'd now be writing what I'm going to tell you. As you know, I've already had some terrible hardships in my life, but I never thought that what I found out at the beginning of this week would happen. A letter that I got from Germany let me know that my father had passed away one-and-a-half months ago. I don't know what to think about this. When I left Munich, I always hoped to see him again—and when I arrived in America, I immediately made plans for a trip to visit him. I just can't grasp the fact that now, when I come back to Germany, I'll go out to the Forest Cemetery. Why did I even travel to America? I wasn't even able to attend the funeral, and I'll never forgive myself for that.

Liselotte suffered a similar loss a few years later, and Ernst tried to console her from afar.

July 1, 1951

Before I write about anything else, I want to share my sincere condolences about your grandmother's death. I can commiserate, of course: I know what it means to lose one of your loved ones, and I ask you to convey my condolences to your parents.

[M]ost of the people bought things without knowing what they were buying...

In the following year Liselotte grappled with the disruptions of the *Währungsreform*—the currency reform. Ludwig Erhard, who directed the Bi-Zonal Economic Administration, introduced this set of policies in 1948 to combat soaring inflation and the thriving black market. Central to his strategy was devaluating the old reichsmark. On June 20, 1948, everyone in the French, American, and British occupation zones was given forty new deutsche marks in exchange for forty of the old reichsmarks; in addition, however, all bank deposits and cash now faced an exchange rate of one hundred reichsmarks for 6.5 new DMs—meaning that bank deposits were now worth only seven percent of their prior value. Although the reform succeeded in the long term by promoting the sale of consumer goods, quashing the black market, and helping to usher in the so-called 1950s Economic Miracle, its immediate effect was to plunge the lives of ordinary Germans into turbulence and uncertainty.

Ernst wanted to find out more about this situation.

June 19, 1948

I just heard a radio report about the introduction of the currency reform in the Western zones of Germany. Please let me know about this.

Almost at the same time Liselotte was writing him about this very topic, focusing on the shopping frenzy that exploded when these economic measures were implemented.

June 18, 1948

Over here things are terrible today; it's completely chaotic and so disorderly that it's impossible to describe. The currency reform! You really can't imagine this at all, and you really can't conceive of how this dampens people's spirits. The first law was already announced on the eight o'clock news; the devaluation followed at 1:10. That's why I want to write a letter to you that's as long as possible, even though it's already gotten late and even though I'm at my wit's end because of how all of the chaos affected things at work. If I send off the letter tomorrow, then it'll still cost fifty pennies—but it'll be five marks compared to my last paycheck. That shows how this reform has gotten off to an awkward start, and it hasn't been easy—so let me pull myself together when I write to you today! I think that the beginning will be incredibly difficult. You only get enough money for life's necessities—no more. You can't even think it all through and make plans. But things have to get back to normal over time—and most of all things need to grow and develop. Because this currency reform is supposed to make our economy healthier, and that's something that we can only hope for. I took time off this afternoon because I still wanted to buy some English books, but I couldn't even get a single one anymore. I was really angry about that, because most of the people bought things without knowing what they were buying, just to "spend" the money! There's a mindless, impulsive mood in the city, and I was glad when I was back home again. The foreigners were especially nasty and "at the top of their game" today!

We'll get forty marks for four weeks—new marks for us to live on...I'm just glad that, because of Miss Reiner's influence, I could buy things that it made sense to buy, even if they were more expensive, because today I wouldn't have been able to use that money for anything at all. Of course, I'll try to write to you often using this new money, but I'll have to wait first to see how things develop. Unfortunately, it's still not possible for me to send you an air mail letter. Maybe it'll soon be possible now, after all of this. As soon as it is, I'll do it—because I'd be so elated myself if I could. Now I have to try to tear myself away from this subject and write to you about other things.

In the same month Liselotte let Ernst know that she needed to be prudent with her expenditures.

I've also already received my first paycheck in the new currency. I was very happy to get a full paycheck after having such a small amount of money (forty marks). In spite of that I still have to watch my pennies because I want to buy various things for myself.

The impact of the currency reform continued to make itself felt a few months later. At the end of September 1948 Liselotte wrote:

Since the currency reform took effect various theaters have had to declare bankruptcy—none of the well-established ones, but some of the newer ones.

The streetcar is now running until 12:30 AM. The ridership at night is supposed to be pretty large, but just don't ask what sorts of people these are, because the real people of Munich naturally aren't all going out yet. Instead it's the racketeers and black-market people—who still exist in spite of the currency reform—who can call the shots now because they can easily afford these prices. You know, of course, how much shoes used to cost here; these days a pair of simple sports shoes in my size costs at least fifty to sixty-five German marks. And this is the situation for almost all consumer goods as well as groceries. I'm just happy that I don't urgently need such things right now, because you can hardly afford them.

"Die Gedanken sind frei."

The most excruciating hardship that confronted Ernst was, by far, the time that he spent doing forced labor at Rothenförde and then at Wolmirsleben. Very little in my parents' files sheds light on these months in 1945, and of course our father himself had remained tight-lipped about what had transpired there.

In the late Seventies I spent two years as a guest student at the state university in Tübingen. One day, while browsing in a bookstore on Naukler Street, I came across the German translation of a book by Helen Epstein called *Children of the Holocaust: Conversations with the Sons and Daughters of Survivors.* Though I bought it right away and paged through parts of it, I've never been able to get through the whole thing systematically, just like I've never extensively combed through the scholarly literature dealing with the Holocaust itself. When I tried to read books like this one, there always came a point when darkness and disquietude overwhelmed me, and I needed to back away, to get some distance from the stark ugliness of what was being the described.

In a general way, though, flipping through portions of the Epstein paperback has made me think, again and again over the years, about how my father's time in labor camps—and, to a lesser extent, my grandmother's ordeal at Theresienstadt—impacted my life and those of my siblings. To some extent, for example, my curiosity about my parents' past led me to study German and master the language. In part I pursued German to recover some of my own past; after all, it had been my initial language when I was growing up. Beyond that, though, I wanted to recover a wider part of my family's history. I yearned to gain fluency in the language so that I could travel to Munich, Straubing, and elsewhere to uncover what their earlier years had actually looked and felt like.

Without my family background I probably never would have become as involved with Amnesty International as I've been. When I was a guest student in Tübingen, I came across AI posters and handbills here and there, and it was there that I began writing letters now and then on behalf of prisoners of conscience in all corners of the globe. Learning what I did about the Holocaust as well as current human rights issues led me to take an active role in Amnesty to the point where, when I did graduate studies in Toronto from 1979 to 1982, I volunteered regularly at the AI office in the Church of the Holy Trinity, a modest building adjacent to the mall at Eaton Centre. I also made AI meetings at the Cumberland House a part of my weekly schedule. A few years later, soon after I moved to Fresno and began teaching at Edison High in 1985, I located a local Amnesty group and wound up leading it for two years. For about a year and a half I also sponsored an AI student group at Edison, though—given the sobering, grim nature of the work—that sputtered out over time. Human rights issues didn't appeal to many high schoolers to begin with; after the original core of interested students graduated, no others appeared to take their place.

My fascination with authors like Fyodor Dostoyevsky probably also stems from my family's Holocaust background. I first came across Dostoyevsky's novels during undergraduate years at the University of the Pacific in Stockton. There, during the fall semester in 1974, I wound up working as a teaching assistant for Professor Leonard O'Bryon when he offered a course in nineteenth-century Russian literature. His syllabus included both *Crime and Punishment* and *The Brothers Karamazov*, and the second of these left an especially strong mark on me. In one early chapter, "Rebellion," Ivan tells his brother Alyosha hideous stories about mistreated and abused children. After reading that section until late into the night, I went to bed, only to be plagued by vivid Karamazov-inspired nightmares. I woke up screaming, and I woke Tom up at the same time.

Only a few years ago I discovered Dostoyevsky's *The House of the Dead*, which intrigued me with its documentary-like portrayal of the author's four-year ordeal in a Siberian labor camp.

I remember seeing Pier Paolo Pasolini's *Salo* in Tübingen soon after it was released in the mid-Seventies. The film's been banned in many countries over the years because of its lurid and extreme brutality; I doubt that I could stomach much of it nowadays, but at that time I was transfixed by it. Using de Sade's *The 120 Days of Sodom* as its inspiration, the movie explored in increasingly unsettling ways just how monstrous the world of the camps must have been. Other, more mainstream films such as *Schindler's List* also became important stepping stones for me as I sought to gain a greater awareness and deeper understanding of the so-called Final Solution.

Sometimes, due my family's background, I've reacted differently to popular entertainment than many of my peers. In one scene in *The Empire Strikes Back* Han Solo is tortured, but the film downplays the moral offensiveness of torture so that the scene fits in easily with the lightweight conventions of a space opera. I was troubled by the way those moments—gruesome and sadistic as they were for me—so readily and breezily trivialized torture, and more recently I've had the same reaction to similar scenes in such cinematic offerings as *Casino Royale* and *Spectre*.

For many years I regularly treated myself to *Law and Order* on Wednesday nights and usually relished its engaging, byzantine storylines, but one episode blindsided and disturbed me. That time the plot centered on a woman whose parents were Holocaust survivors; her parents' past had rendered her so distraught and unstable that she wound up killing someone. Here, to my mind, the reality of the Holocaust was once again trivialized and made superficial. It was just grist for the mill of a crime show plot, something offbeat that might appeal to a certain demographic of viewers.

How did Ernst deal with his experiences in Wolmirsleben? How did he cope with the savagery that he'd endured and the scars that they'd left inside? Much of the answer to that is beyond my reach now. As I wrote earlier, he'd meticulously kept a private journal for several decades, but my mother had opted to burn it soon after he passed. The profound joy he reaped from his early skiing and hiking adventures helped him to do battle with the grim shadows inside, to be sure. Later on he took us on hikes and fishing expeditions in the Sierras, and those probably acted as a tonic of sorts as well. His love of music certainly had a palliative role. His religious faith was crucial, as was his deep-seated conviction that all problems and challenges could be confronted head-on and overcome with sustained effort. His wartime experiences probably caused the insomnia that occasionally plagued him, but pacing around the house in those hushed early morning hours might also have helped him out. It could have been a boon for him to confront demons from the past in solitude, to grapple with them and weaken their hold on him.

Beyond that, though, a Sixties television series salved and raised his spirits to no end, and that show was *Hogan's Heroes*. If memory serves, he watched that CBS sitcom religiously every week that it was on the air, and every week he laughed boisterously at the assorted antics of Colonel Hogan and his POW sidekicks. After all, without fail Hogan and his intrepid band always managed to turn the tables on their bungling German captors at Stalag 13. Indeed, they always got the better of them, whether by accessing clandestine tunnels or bribing low-level German officers. My father's favorite character in the cast, by a long shot, was the obese and teddy bear-lovable Sergeant Schultz, the recipient of many such bribes and a pushover for abject flattery. The show's cast probably never intended this to happen, but their banter and shenanigans proved to be a balm and a tonic for our father. I don't recall him ever be as relaxed or as boyishly amused as he was during those weekly visits with the gang at Stalag 13.

What else helps to explain how he could rise above the darkness of his past? Other factors would include the acceptance and support that he found at Super Mold, the chance to apply himself to challenging technical problems—and, in a related way, the time that he spent in the U.S. Army. He told me once that in the Army he was judged for what he was and what he could do. He wasn't pigeonholed and condemned as a *Mischling* for being half Jewish, as had happened before.

My mother, though she hadn't been sent to a camp, also suffered many hardships in the course of her childhood and early adulthood. What sustained and inspired her? How is it that, like my father, she learned to rise above her past and move beyond it? So many photo albums that Tom and I uncovered in the family house show two genuinely happy faces, glowing with vitality and verve, with a jubilant energy. Much of what fueled my father's spirits played a role in my mother's psyche as well, to be sure. The bond of love and devotion that they had was clearly central. But here another memory emerges for me, and curiously enough it has to do with another television show—this time an ABC made-for-TV movie that aired in 1971 called *The Birdmen*. In it a group of intrepid POWs are held at Beckstadt Castle, a reputedly inescapable prison. Surreptitiously, however, they construct a glider, and toward the end of the film one of them successfully uses it to make his getaway. As he does, the song *"Die Gedanken sind frei"* plays in the soundtrack. After we watched the film, both of our parents told us about that song. It clearly had a profound meaning for them.

Its opening stanza reveals its core message:

Thoughts are free—who can tell what they are?
They fly by like shadows in the night.
No one can guess what they are, no hunter can shoot them
with powder and lead. Thoughts are free!

And so in the fourth stanza the persona resolves to live his life accordingly.

So from now on I'll give up all of my sorrows
and never again will I hector myself with foolish things.
In your heart you can always laugh and joke, and you
and can tell yourself at the same time: Thoughts are free!

During its long history the song's often been associated with protest against political repression and subjugation—in the age of Metternich in 19th-century Austria, for example. When they spoke with us after we'd finished watching *The Birdmen*, though, our parents didn't have that sort of historical era in mind. For them the lyrics meant just one thing—that, despite what's happening around you, you can always find solace and serenity inside your own mind, and you can always treasure your own thoughts.

When I look now at my parents' beaming faces—in their engagement photos, in their reunion pictures of 1951, in the pictures of their early Lodi years—I realize that those can't just be taken for granted. Both of them took pains to cultivate a strong, vibrant inner life that kept the events around them at arm's length—first as a means of living through the Third Reich and then, later on, to cope with the trials of postwar Germany. Finally, they drew on the same strategy to deal with the challenges of settling in another country and coming to terms with its social and cultural norms and expectations. This mental stance that they sought to make their own reminds me of the stoicism of Marcus Aurelius, the Roman emperor and philosopher. In his *Meditations* he mused, for example, that "[v]ery little is needed to make a happy life; it's all within yourself, in your way of thinking."

Lodi / California, 1. März 1947.

Liebes Fräulein Peschel!

Herzlichsten Dank für Ihren so lieben Brief. Nun, wie geht es Ihnen? Sie schreiben zwar gut, jedoch nehme ich an, daß es unter den gegebenen Verhältnissen in mancher Richtung nicht gerade zum Besten ist. Wie sieht denn z.B. Ihre Wohnungslage aus? Wie geht es im Geschäft?

Ich bin soweit gesund. Californien ist ein wunderschönes Land und ich könnte Ihnen viel erzählen. Aber alles hat nicht Platz in einem Brief. Meine Arbeit ist meine größte Freude. Einige von mir konstruierten, unwohligen Maschinen sind bereits fertig. Bis jetzt war noch alles O.K., was der Deutschländer machte. Vor 3 Monaten wurde ich zum Junior-Ingenieur ernannt. Vor einiger Zeit sagte ich mein Chef, daß ich sein zweitbester Ingenieur sei. Bei mir im Büro spricht niemand deutsch und so muß ich den ganzen Tag englisch reden. Ich komme schon recht gut zurecht, nur meine Aussprache macht den Amerikanern manchmal Schwierigkeiten. Ich bin ja so froh, weil ich die Möglichkeit habe, in meinem Beruf zu arbeiten. Deutsch komme ich nur am Abend zu meiner Mutter sprechen. Dies ist der Jammer, weil ich Ihren Brief nicht in englisch beantworte. Ich habe ja ohne

CHAPTER SEVEN

America

An ocean voyage like this is wonderful...

*P*eriodically Ernst shared his thoughts about the United States with his Liselotte. At first this was probably because of the vivid and deep impressions that his new homeland made on him—in particular, the rugged beauty of the Sierra Nevada mountain range. Beyond that, he strove to quench her thirst for information about this exotic location. Later on, as his hopes for a long-term relationship grew stronger and more conceivable, he seemed to write about this topic with a view toward preparing her for what would await her should she actually come out to California and live with him.

His train ride across the continental U.S. filled him with vivid impressions that he was bursting to share.

September 15, 1946

Oh, I could write so much to you, because during my long trip I saw so many new things. I was seasick for two of the ten days that we needed to cross the Atlantic. An ocean voyage like this is wonderful, and I hope that you'll also have the luck to take a similar trip someday. I spent my first six weeks in America in New York. When I was in this gigantic city, I never stopped being amazed. It took several days for me just to grasp that I was now really standing on American soil. But the English-speaking population—which I had a very difficult time communicating with—proved to me again and again that I was actually here, not to mention the grocery stores and the department stores filled with merchandise. A speedy modern train brought me to the West in three days' time. The trip across the entire breadth of America was very interesting and colorful. Now I'm here in a modern town in California. As opposed to the skyscrapers, subways, and overhead trains of New York, here there are palm trees, nut and fig trees, and also prodigious amounts of fruit.

Of course, it's really hot; there's no rain at all during the summer. Less appealing to me is the fact that there's no snow during the winter, and soon winter will be here again. Since I found work in my field in a machine factory, I'm even happier here. But, please don't think that America's a land of milk and honey. You know, it's not always easy when you live in a foreign country. I'm very homesick a lot of the time, and I pine for Munich.

Liselotte, for her part, pelted Ernst with questions about his new town and its environs.

March 17, 1947

Where is this place called "Lodi" actually located? I've already looked at the map a few times, but I haven't found it yet. How big is it? I mean, about how many people live there?...Is it expensive for you there?

She was especially interested in the customs and traditions that Ernst had come across.

Do you also celebrate Easter? It's a silly question, but I really don't know how things are in Lodi! If you do celebrate it…then enjoy yourself and have fun!

Sometimes she leveled a lengthy set of scattershot questions at him.

June 11, 1947

I also wanted to ask you about the time difference and how it works. As of yesterday we have "double summer time"—that is, two hours before the normal summer time. How does that square with your time? When it's eight o'clock here, how late is it where you are? I'd really like to know if the time difference is larger or smaller now.

How long is your work day? Do you also have to work on Saturday? I'm glad that we have Saturdays off. I'd also like to know what you always do when you're not at work…Have you already been in San Francisco once— or somewhere else? Was it beautiful there? Hey – I'm not curious at all, am I?

Later on, Ernst landed on an original way of determining the time difference between their cities.

November 28, 1948

You asked me about the exact time difference, but I don't know what it is. I don't know how it is during the summer. Maybe we can still figure it out. Check this out: recently there was news on the radio about the birth of the English prince, and the news bulletin mentioned that the prince had been born at 9:15 in England, which corresponds to 2:15 Pacific Summer Savings Time according to the San Francisco station. And so the time difference between Lodi and London is seven hours. Now, if you can find out if the time in England currently corresponds to the time in Germany, or if you can find out what the difference is, then maybe we can finally figure out the answer to this.

Everything from the weather to American cars piqued Liselotte's curiosity.

July 23, 1947

I can really believe it when you write that the constant beautiful weather also gets to be monotonous. And above all the heat…Here where we are the weather's constantly changing. It's too bad that, as soon as it rains, it cools down so much right away, and mostly the rain doesn't stop anymore.

February 27, 1948

Please tell me again about your life in your new country so that I can better imagine what things look like where you are. Americans have such marvelous cars! Here I always see them on the road—they're just wonderful! Many German girls are allowed to ride in them—but it's better not to! I've already peaked into one once that was parked along the street close to us. The things on the dashboard are really arranged well, and the car has a comfortable steering wheel. All in all, to sum it up in a word—magnificent! Can you often drive with a car like that? Here lots of people are driving them!

At times she couldn't refrain from offering her criticisms about some American customs.

March 18, 1948

Thanks so much for providing your description of America. It's very interesting to hear about that, but it was also really hard for me to read about. But I can certainly understand that you still enjoy German cuisine a lot more. But, you know, it bothers me that those people over there in America, your new home, only eat with their forks. Over here, doing that really isn't considered good table manners. But—other countries, other customs!

On occasion Ernst included some show-and-tell items about the New World with his letters.

March 27, 1948

Tomorrow is Easter Sunday. Unfortunately we don't have Good Friday and Easter Monday as holidays here. The twig that I've enclosed belonged to a consecrated American palm, and I got it last Sunday (Palm Sunday) in church.

I'm also enclosing a newspaper clipping that deals with California. I've already seen all of the places mentioned in the article many times. They aren't great cities, but rather places which are important for historical reasons. Personally, I don't like Jackson. There you run across so many drunks, and there aren't many authentic [in English] *Westerners (old timers)* [in German] *to see there.*

The Bay Area fired Ernst's enthusiasm. As an engineer, he was especially taken by the technical majesty of the bridges there.

May 3, 1948

Today, though, I want to chat with you a little more about America. Last Saturday I was in San Francisco again. You've certainly heard about the big bridge that connects Oakland with San Francisco. It's really a marvelous structure. Just imagine: the traffic flows on two different levels. The passenger cars drive on the upper story—three lanes in each direction, and there's always one car right behind the other in this endless stream of traffic. Half of the lower story is reserved for trucks; the streetcar runs on the other half. I can't tell you exactly how long the bridge is because I don't know that myself. But, anyway, it's really very big. Maybe you can get a sense of it if I tell you that four painters are busy every day painting the bridge. When they've finished up at one end, then the other end's already starting to rust. No pedestrians are allowed on the bridge. From a technical perspective, you really have to admire this feat of engineering. Just imagine: the entire structure is just hanging on cables. I haven't been on the Golden Gate Bridge yet; the way it's constructed is only different from the Bay Bridge in one way—its piers are more distant from one another than those of any other bridge in the world.

When we took road trips as a family, our father—always the person behind the wheel—was often eager to comment on the bridges that we traversed. Usually this fascination with the structure of the manmade world was one of his benign quirks, but sometimes, given his passion for such things, it went way overboard. Once, when we were seated in a fine San Francisco restaurant, all set for the waiter to arrive and take our orders, he peered curiously at the table and then at our chairs. Then his curiosity got the better of him, and he couldn't resist standing up, lifting his own chair way over his head, and examining the way that its legs were attached to the rest of it.

Liselotte took the trouble to do some research about one of the bridges that he'd mentioned.

Steven Roesch

May 12, 1948

In your dear letter you told me once again about various things over in America. I knew about some of them already, and some of them were new to me. Just now I wanted to tell you how long the bridge is. I actually have a small book here that describes the most significant and largest structures in the world, but I'd have to dig it out. (It's buried under several other books.) That'd take too long for me now, but I think that the bridge is thirty-six kilometers long—though I can't absolutely guarantee that this is correct.

In the 1940s Lodi boasted a flourishing wine industry, as it still does to this day.

September 15, 1948

Today we had the first cool day in months. The thermometer went down to seventy degrees Fahrenheit. This is very bad for the grapes, and the grape harvest will already be late this year as it is. Next weekend there'll be the annual [in English] *"Grape and Winter Festival"* [in German] *in Lodi.*

Ernst's engineering expertise informed the way he described the apartment where he and Amalie lived.

November 25, 1948

The house that I live in isn't a brick house; it's made out of wood. Still, the outer and inner walls are masonry and (please excuse this comment) you definitely wouldn't notice the difference. You know, the building techniques are just different in America, and the reason for these techniques in California has to do primarily with heat-technological advantages. (The houses cool down quickly at sunset. On the other hand, bricks, if they're solid, will absorb heat during the day and then release that heat during the coolness of the night, and a house would then be a furnace all the time.) But that's enough of that, otherwise I'd have to write down the entire history of American building techniques. (Skyscrapers are, naturally, not built out of wood!)

If you're laughing about me now and saying that I live in a wooden shack, then I can tell you in all honesty that it's the most beautiful and modern place that I've ever lived in.

So I've got to send my mother out to buy beer for me.

Ernst also let Liselotte know about some Americans' cliché-ridden views of Germany and the Germans.

March 2, 1948

My colleagues always tease me because I come from Munich, and over the past twelve years the city of Munich has gotten a reputation in which "beer" plays a prominent role. I'll just provide a few excerpts from an American encyclopedia:

[in English] *"Bavaria. Bavaria is the largest beer-producing country in the world, and the beer is its most important manufactured product."*

"Munich is one of the finest towns in Germany. Brewing is the chief industry."

[in German] *My colleagues always want to know if I was raised with on bottles of beer. All of them like it when I tell them about the Hofbräuhaus... and they'd all like to see a liter-sized beer mug, the kind of mug that all of the soldiers stationed in Munich have been talking about. Something like that doesn't exist here at all, but when you imagine the prodigious amount of beer that's swimming in these liter-sized mugs at the moment...Actually, I shouldn't even be drinking any beer here, because I'm not twenty-one years old yet. So I've got to send my mother out to buy beer for me.*

It took a while for Ernst to get used to the intense summer heat in the Central Valley.

June 24, 1948

Now it's awfully hot here again. This makes it harder to work, and even at my type of job at the drawing board, which doesn't require much physical exertion, I'm sweating from early in the day until the evening. Sometimes I have to change my shirt twice on the same day. But you get used to it. When the days are especially hot, I have to think back on Miss Reiner's very cool office, where we had to do our work dressed in winter coats, hats, and gloves. Can you also still remember how it was? Now I remember that back then you had such an attractive coat with a hood, one that I always really liked.

He was also candid about the social distinctions that he observed in Lodi—for example, those that informed New Year's Eve celebrations.

December 31, 1947

Right now it's New Year's Eve—that is, it's about eight o'clock. Naturally, everyone here is eagerly waiting for the New Year to begin. Why is it this way? We were allowed to leave work two hours early so that we could make the best use of the rest of the old year. When you think about such festivities in America, you might be imagining something very special. In America some traditional customs are certainly honored here and there, but overall the event is the same as in Germany: it's a colorful public display. But then again this doesn't hold true everywhere, because what people drink or whether they drink at all completely depends on the individual family. The really big celebrations, what Germans imagine American New Year's Eve celebrations to be like, only happen in night clubs, where tickets (which include food) cost up to a hundred dollars each. That's something that I could never afford, of course. However, I'll be going to the movies at ten o'clock, because people have told me that this is also something special—a midnight show. I'll tell you about it later on.

Liselotte wasn't altogether enthusiastic about his depiction of an American-style *Sylvester.*

January 10, 1948

I'm actually disappointed that all of you don't celebrate New Year's Eve better....Apparently, where you are, there are just the really big, expensive celebrations and nothing else. For the other people—for the mere mortals— that's out of the question. You know, I wouldn't like that. By the way, there aren't supposed to be class distinctions where you are.

148

Ernst also noted stark differences between the culinary preferences in California and those of his Bavarian homeland.

November 13, 1948

When I snack on peanuts and a coke at work, just like my colleagues, then I remember the many black bread rolls that I wanted back then, and often you gave me the bread tickets for them. I've repeatedly told people at work about the dark rolls—and the people in Munich would certainly laugh at me if they found out that nowadays I'm snacking on peanuts. Sometimes I bring a real butter-topped roll from home, and even my co-workers admit that it's not bad. Still, they prefer to eat a candy bar.

When he considered the earnings that an average American worker could expect to receive, he revealed some of his own priorities.

November 25, 1948

All right, so what's average salary that an American gets? Now, you believe that it's $5,000 because that's what you read in a magazine. Whether that's right or not, I'll say up front that this is just one publisher's opinion, that another magazine can publish other opinions, and that both are false and correct in some cases. It really completely depends on the nature of these statistics. Where do they come from? How? In which state? About which social class? You'll have to admit that these factors would lead to different figures; that even more "statistical fuzziness" could be expected in cheap magazine articles; and that it's often just an author's opinion. That's why you read various newspapers here and you develop your own opinion. To get a more accurate answer for you, I asked several colleagues, and here's the answer that all of them gave: [in English] *"If five thousand dollar [sp] is the average, then I'm under average."* [in German] *I'd say, and this is just my view, that $2500 is the average annual income of an American—and here I'm not talking about the so-called captains of industry. It's true that the salary doesn't rise in proportion with the amount of formal education that you have. Here it's this way: you need to be satisfied with the joy that comes from your work, because a big title definitely doesn't earn you any money—that's to say* *that it doesn't determine the amount of your salary. I personally would never give up my career for a few dollars because I enjoy my work, because I find a purpose for my life in my work.*

Ernst also commented on significant differences between the educational systems in Germany and in the States.

July 29, 1948

If...I look at the life of an American student, then I notice things that you and I never experienced. Seen superficially, it's like this: we actually just went to school to learn, and in our way of thinking this was completely normal and proper. By contrast, American students—because of a different school system—have a good time at school. Of course, I can't go into all of the particulars here, but just imagine—every school has its own tennis courts, swimming pools, basketball courts, and baseball and football stadiums so that the sports facilities connected with the school building are larger than the actual school building itself. I'd also like to say that the American school system also differs from its German counterpart in that here you go to elementary school [Volksschule] for eight years and then to [in English] high school [in German] for three years—although the final year of high school isn't mandatory. You can only start career training after completing high school, and to this end you go to a college and, in some cases, maybe to the university later on. Of course, here there isn't the type of fundamental instruction in trades that Germany has, because that sort of apprenticeship system doesn't exist in America. Still, many specialized courses are available, and so there's the opportunity to really learn a lot; it depends entirely on the student's motivation. By no means are enjoyable activities in short supply; for example, there are regular teenage clubs which organize weekly dances. [in English, preserving Ernst's misspelling] *Teen-ager* [in German] *are students who are between* [numbers in English] *thir*teen *and nine*teen *years old.* [in German] *In Germany you could, in some situations, be expelled from school if, as a thirteen-year-old, you went to a dance with a girl—isn't that true? There's never a shortage of festive events here, and so I really have to emphasize that* [in English] *"These kids are having a good time."*

Needless to say, Ernst preferred the political system in the United States to what'd he'd suffered through earlier. He also cherished the openness and tolerance that many Americans exhibited.

July 29, 1948

It seems to me that you've been hearing a lot about democracy. I think that in practice this might differ from the way a newspaper and similar things tend to describe it. I'd like to go into more detail and analyze the way life looks when so-called democratic principles are invoked, but I just can't find the right words to do this. Anyway, it's like this: here you have every freedom available, and you are, so to speak, left to your own devices. This system is definitely fundamentally different from the Nazi system, and we're all convinced that the latter system was neither good nor just. For example, your national origins hardly matter at all here in America as long as you behave decently. Of course, if you have trouble with the English language, then that can lead to difficulties at work, etc., but in your private life an odd pronunciation—something that always marks you as an immigrant—definitely doesn't make waves. People don't look down on you because of this. In this respect Americans are definitely very tolerant. Of course, my colleagues tease me now and then when I sometimes make mistakes in English. However, if you don't ask Americans to correct your mistakes, they'll never do it on their own. That's only something immigrants who have been here for a while will do, because they want to make themselves look important.

He also assured Liselotte that serious concert music had a large following in central California.

July 29, 1948

And now some words about American music, something which you apparently don't like much at all. Please don't be angry, my dear Liselotte, but probably the type of American music that you hear is stuff that many natural-born Americans wouldn't like. Aside from the foolish noise, as you call it—which is probably music that comes from the Southern states—there are very nice folk songs, operettas, and concert works here. The so-called love songs come in a wide spectrum of moods, and their melodies sometimes resemble those of their German counterparts—unless, of course, they've been "jazzed up" by various orchestras and have thus lost their original shape. Here songs such as "Rosamunde, You Can't Be True" and "In the Evening on the Heath" are played with American texts; this certainly proves that they match up with American tastes...The music of Vienna as well as demanding music of Beethoven, Wagner, Schubert, Mozart, etc. are performed here a lot, and they're very popular. Overall, Americans have a great interest in serious music, and these sorts of music lovers have a high regard for German music, in particular the works of Beethoven and Wagner. Of course, here you can also listen to Italian, Spanish, and South American music—and actually all sorts of music—not only jazz, as you might believe.

Of course, Ernst conceded, his views about the two countries might only have limited validity.

July 29, 1948

Ever since I've been in America I've tried to observe what's new around me and to compare all of that with my homeland. Unfortunately I can't do this completely, because I never knew "Germany in normal times." Beyond that, during my time in Germany I was never given equal treatment—except during the time after the war.

One pound of coffee = a half-hour in the case of an average American worker.

Three years later, after Ernst had entered the U.S. Army and been sent to Europe, he shared his thoughts about post-war Germany with Liselotte.

July 7, 1951

Now I want to let you know a little about my impressions. In economic terms this country has really recovered wonderfully. It's really admirable. In spite of that, however, the prices, especially prices for everyday necessities, are sky-high, in my opinion. I'm comparing an hour of work in Germany, paid in German marks, with the buying power that the hour has. The upshot is that there's a much lower living standard compared to the one in America. But there are really first-rate stores, restaurants, and entertainment venues here which charge ridiculously high prices just as in the United States, and that proves that someone (outside of the Americans) must be buying. Otherwise all of these businesses would go bankrupt. Until someone can explain this better to me, there's just one way that I can account for it. In America there's everything for everyone who makes an effort. Here there's everything (yes, maybe even somewhat better quality), but actually just for the big shots. Once you asked me—it was years ago in a letter—whether it was true that there's no class distinction in the U.S.A. It's only today, after I've seen Germany again, that I feel that I'm in a position to give a legitimate answer.

In terms of appearance: <u>no</u>;

In terms of finances: <u>yes</u>; but, after all, there's everything from a beggar to a millionaire everywhere.

In terms of the standard of living?

Here are some examples, and you can make your own comparisons:

A pair of nylon stockings = two hours of work in the case of the most poorly paid female American worker. (For poor-quality stockings this would be one hour of work.)

One pound of coffee = a half-hour in the case of an average American worker.

A pack of cigarettes (twenty cigarettes) = one-tenth of an hour of work (six minutes) in the case of the most poorly paid temporary worker in America.

A man's suit, depending on its quality, could be purchased with about sixty hours of work.

How this compares to a German worker, who has to work for less pay, is something that you can figure out on your own.

Maybe you're wondering why I'm writing about such simple products. Here's the reason. From what I've seen, luxury items cost less in Germany than in the U.S.A. (clocks, jewelry, porcelain, etc.). But how can you think about things like these when all of your income is frittered away to buy life's necessities? What follows from this is that luxury articles *are just for those earning a lot and those who can make purchases with money that they've earned. (One dollar equals 4.20 German marks.) For the rest of the population, for example, for the diligent German craftsman, such things are only manageable to a very limited extent. So far my letter is giving the impression that I only prefer the U.S.A. when it comes to material goods. No, I introduced these examples because they might give an answer to your question about whether I'd be even able to provide for a wife. Do you remember? We corresponded about this about a year ago.*

Let's go on to something else: you know that it was very hard for me at the beginning of my life in the U.S.A. Getting started and getting used to things wasn't easy, and it took quite a while. It might be that the most recent letters that you got from me from the U.S.A. showed signs of residual homesickness.

Since then I've had the chance to see Germany again. Many of the beautiful things that I thought I'd remembered about Germany just weren't here the way my yearning had conjured them up from far away. Many things disappointed me, even the few lovely memories that I'd taken with me to the U.S.A.

Today I'm homesick for [in English] *California,* [in German] *a place where I've lived for a relatively short time. Why is it that way? Maybe we'll talk about that at some point, but now I can't find the right words to express myself. Probably the same process will happen to you in spite of everything that I'm telling you today. When we've reached our goal at last, when we've set up a home in America and we're happy there, then you probably won't be convinced until at some point we return to visit Germany together and you experience what I'm going through right now. Only then will you understand America in all of its beauty.*

Yes, my dear, it's strange how you can feel "at home" in a foreign country, even though you'll never be able to speak its language without an accent. But without a doubt the U.S.A. is the only country where something like this is magnanimously tolerated. Of course, there are also exceptions; there are people who are very small-minded. But this small group of people just doesn't behave democratically. (I was trying to avoid using that last word, but now it's actually slipped through my pen and onto the paper.) So how are things in this regard in Germany?

As their correspondence continued, and as the bond that embraced them deepened, the tone of their letters changed accordingly.

Lodi, California, 24. Oktober 1948.

Geliebte Liselotte!

Nachfolgende Verse entstammen an einem
einsamen Oktoberabend, den ich in Gedanken
ganz bei Dir verbrachte. Somit sind sie
auch nur für Dich bestimmt und werden
noch heute die Reise zu Dir, meinem
Liebling, antreten.

Einst verließ ich meine Heimat
Es ist schon viel's mehr mein's
Die Welt wollt ich beschen,
was wär' schon zu bereuen. —

So, zog ich in die Ferne
wollt vergessen was einst war,
Neu anfangen und frisch beginnen
so lautete mein Plan. —

Bald drauf war ich in New-York,
einer Stadt wo's alles gab
was so lang ich mußt entbehren
ich in Hüll' und Füll' nun sah.

CHAPTER EIGHT

Love

Still, with every day that I had to spend there, my will to live grew stronger...

Although Ernst and Liselotte had met when they both worked at Therese Reiner's telephone company and became acquainted there, no romance blossomed between them at that time. Nor was a romantic relationship kindled in the immediate wake of the war, when Ernst returned to Munich after surviving his ordeal at Wolmirsleben and, knocking on Therese Reiner's front door, found Liselotte standing in front of him.

Instead, their relationship took root and flourished in the course of their correspondence, nurtured by his stubborn and seemingly unrealistic hopes and then, in the course of time, by her growing conviction that fate itself, as ratified by Herr Bachmaier's astrological insights, called on her to throw in her lot with Ernst Roesch in California.

Beyond their shared anecdotes and observations about music, nature, their ongoing educational and career aspirations, and their hardships, their correspondence offers some understanding of their deepening respect and affection for one another.

In an undated letter tucked away in the 1948 folder Liselotte recalled their interactions on the job at Therese Reiner's firm.

You write that we've known each other for four years. You're right in terms of the amount of time, because I came to Miss Reiner's firm on April 1, 1944. I also know that we got along well with each other and that I liked you as a colleague. And the other things that I did for you—I mean, when I helped you out—that was because I felt sorry for you after all that you had to deal with. It was only a short time ago that I had to laugh to myself. I was thinking about the times when I was making photocopies, and I was happy that you helped me out when it wasn't working for me, or when I asked you if the copy was good enough. Once I was also able to sketch spring sets. It was definitely nice in the Reiner firm. Now the only one of us girls who's still there is Lore-Lies. All of the others are gone.

During the late Forties, in the initial phase of their courtship, they couldn't share time with each other directly. Rather, they shared and traded words—experiences and observations rendered in thoughtfully, sometimes painstakingly constructed letters. The conversations that ensued between them usually spanned several letters, always interrupted by the temporal gaps due to mail delivery and, many times, the work of official censors. As Ernst was keen to observe, the experiences they shared in earlier times provided a foundation for their evolving epistolary friendship.

July 29, 1948

If I'm now living among Americans, then you may easily understand that in the middle of all of these new impressions I often focus on memories, and...I believe that our friendship has grown and developed because of them.

In an undated letter from 1948 Liselotte recalled how she helped him prepare for his appointment at the Gestapo headquarters.

I still remember very well how I packed your suitcase and fastened the cover on top of it, and then you said to me, am I happy that you're leaving, seeing that I'm packing up everything so well, and when you said these words you looked at me in such a sad way. But I know exactly that your comment about packing the suitcase was supposed to be "gallows humor." But now that's enough time writing about things that aren't that that nice.

Hampering their prospects for a life together was not only their distance from each other but also the uncertainty of the postwar world order. At times the outbreak of new hostilities seemed inevitable and even imminent, something that deeply troubled Liselotte.

March 18, 1948

Now for a serious topic—our current, critical situation. What's happening where you are? Truman's speech was very good; I heard the translation. You know, it'd be awful if something like that happened again, and if all of us had to take part in it again. I don't want to think about it.

When he considered what the future might hold for him, Ernst displayed a readiness to accept whatever he might have to face.

April 26, 1948

You heard President Truman's speech. Well, then you know what's happening; I don't know any more myself. Of course, I'll also have to report for military service at some point; I was already examined for military duty within the first month of my arrival here. You also write that in Germany there's a widespread fear of war. Don't be afraid at all on my account, dear Liselotte; something like that can't stop people like you and me. Up to this point I've never written about it, and now I'm happy, on one hand, that you mentioned it in your letter.

All of us hope for the best, of course, but if things develop a different way, then please don't forget me, even if you don't hear from me for a long time. You've already wondered if I might visit you as an American soldier; that would actually be a stroke of luck in the middle of misfortune. If that happened, would you make an exception and fraternize with an "Ami" [German slang for "American"]? Then we'd be able to talk with each other.

After the Soviets blocked all road, rail, and water access to Berlin from the West, the United States and Great Britain started to bring food and other needed supplies to Berlin by air on June 26, 1948. News about this development reached media outlets in Lodi, and they got the attention of Ernst as well as his co–workers.

September 15, 1948

This week I'm still waiting for one of your letters, which are always so sweet, but today I still want to begin to write at least a short letter to you. I hope that you're doing well and that you're in the best of health when these words reach you. Over here all of us are hearing quite a bit of news, especially about the situation in Berlin. My colleagues often ask me, [in English] *"Ernest, how would you like to be in Germany now?"*

For Liselotte, the events in Berlin were so grim that she wanted to avoid contemplating them altogether.

Sept 30, 1948

Regarding the Berlin situation, there's an article in the newspaper that says that there's no possibility of getting along peacefully with the Russians, and that we should give up trying to do that…What do people say about that where you are? Many people here believe that the Americans will then leave us in the lurch. I shouldn't even think about such things, because I'd start getting very worried right away, and we can't do anything to change any of that.

Despite such political developments Ernst's hopes usually continued to burn bright. Over time his rhetoric bore witness to his deepening affection for Liselotte and his appreciation for the support and care that she showed toward him.

At the same time he strove to be honest and transparent with her about his shortcomings, including an inner disquiet that occasionally took hold of him.

September 20, 1948

I finally got mail from you again. At work today all that I could think about was my mailbox at home, and luckily I wasn't disappointed this time.

So, many affectionate thanks for your letter of the twelfth of this month. Once again you wrote so sweetly and, as always, you're so good to me. The way you sympathize with me when I tell you about my troubles is especially touching, and I can sense how you really support me and what you think about me. It's really wonderful for me to know a kind person like you. I don't even know if it's at all right for me to burden you with all of my problems at work, etc., but, you know, I really trust you a lot and, given all of my plans for the future, I'd rather let you know about all of these unpleasant things now. If I didn't do this, then you might be disappointed when, later on, you have to deal with an Ernst who's in a bad mood. Say, can you imagine this—how it will be then with us in the future? Oh, please, write me about that. I'd really be happy to read about it.

His conviction that they'd share their lives together found its deepest and most direct expression when he let her know about how he'd survived his time at Wolmirsleben. Given his ardent Catholicism, their eventual union in marriage was, in his view, nothing less than part of a divinely ordained plan.

October 7, 1948

You wrote about the widespread talk in Germany about the tense political situation. Over here it's not all that different. But whatever might come in the future, my love, this doesn't really have to mean that "your Ernst, who is faithful to you" will just have been a few lines of ink at some point. I just want to tell you that, when the Gestapo sent me to the camp back then, I never thought that I'd survive, even if I did say "Until we see each other again" [Auf Wiedersehen] to you. Still, with every day that I had to spend there, my will to live grew stronger, and the fact that I did survive proves that our dear Lord determines who may live—and not a Himmler nor a Hitler. And it will be this way in the future, and even if (I think that I can put this down on paper, because you already read about it in the newspaper) it comes to a third world war, this won't ever determine whether you'll be mine or not—because this is also God's will and the fate that He arranges. I'm only writing this because you commented: "In that case we couldn't think about seeing each other again." Of course we all need to do whatever we can if we want to achieve something, because if you or I did nothing and passively trusted the power of fate, that would certainly be the wrong way to interpret God's providence. I hope that you really understand what I'm saying, and that you look forward to what is to come and stand by what is to come, the way that I do.

...but you only know me through my writing, and that's too little.

At times Liselotte was taken aback by the amount of affection that his words displayed. Once, when one of his letters included a particular term of endearment for the first time, she asked him to stop using it.

January 6, 1948

But before I tell you about what's been happening with me, I want to thank you for your nice birthday wishes and your pretty card. It arrived fairly early, but you didn't forget about my birthday. I was very happy about that. Regarding what you added for the first time—you know what I'm referring to—I ask you to refrain from doing this in the future.

She admonished him about a related topic just a few days later.

January 10, 1948

So, once again, you're making plans. I've already mentioned this to you a few times now. You shouldn't do that. Things can develop in a completely different way, and most of all it doesn't make sense it to make plans like these. So, please, follow my advice and think about it. Thanks once again for your nice wishes for 1948.

In one undated letter from 1948 she wrote to him at length about the feelings he was nurturing for her. She wasn't *angry or upset,* she let him know, *but I'm just thinking about it...If you actually came here today, we still don't know if we'd understand each other very well and if we'd be suited for each other. That's also the big question that writing alone can't answer. You also understand that yourself, as you've written to me already.*

You yourself, I feel, think that we'd be a good match, but you only know me through my writing, and that's too little. I'm naturally writing without whitewashing anything, but what's written down sounds like something that's spoken aloud. Yes, dear Ernst, I have to say it again, that we only know each other—and parted company—as colleagues at work, and I've already written once to you that if we were to meet we'd just have to skip over all of these years when we've corresponded and become good friends. I think that might not be so hard for you, but I imagine that it wouldn't be that easy for me. I don't know, but when I think about it and try to picture it, then it doesn't seem all that easy to me.

She assured him that, had he proclaimed his feelings for her when they'd both worked for Frau Reiner, he would have been immediately rebuffed.

I think it was more sensible that you never said anything like that to me. I actually would have been very offended. I was actually very sensitive, as a matter of fact, and I never would have understood that at all. It might actually be more difficult to understand me than other young women in this respect, at least a majority of them. I think that it was good that you didn't make your feelings known back then.

Dear Ernst, I understand your sentiments very well, but as I've now mentioned many times, I don't want to make you any promises—something that you, as I know you, will certainly understand the right way.

It took a while for Ernst to convince Liselotte that they should write to one another using the "du" form of address—the form used between family members and close friends. He noted that Miss Detl, another woman who'd worked in the Reiner firm, had opted to speak with him this way. Liselotte responded to his recollections in another 1948 letter.

Now, about calling each other "du" during the time we worked for Frau Reiner. Here I can only say that this never would have happened—starting to use the casual "du" with you so quickly. I'm not the sort of person who would do that; I don't know any other way to explain this. The situation involving Miss Detl was an odd one, because we actually didn't have a reason to call you "du" as soon as we met you. She probably had another opinion about this, and I'm glad that you were holding yourself back, because I would have been very sensitive about this—and maybe this would have been foolish of me, but that's just the way it is. Back then you did the right thing by not saying a thing about it, because that wouldn't have been good. It's just nice that you remember all of that.

In the following month, however, she did eventually agree that they'd henceforth address each more informally. It might be that she'd had a chance to pour over Herr Bachmaier's astrological observations around this time; maybe this accounts for her change of heart and rhetorical style.

February 27, 1948

How are things actually going with you, dear Ernst? Now you've already been gone from here for such a long time. I think that we really don't know each other at all anymore—it's been so long since we saw each other the last time! I often think about how things came to be this way. Back then you were with the Reiner firm, and then you were sent away [to the labor camp], *and then suddenly you were gone, completely gone, away from here, into another world; and if we're totally honest with each other, then we've only been writing—or more to the point we've been conversing—since you left here, even though you wrote quite a bit before then. I still have a card that you sent to me from the* [Wolmirsleben] *camp, and also the nice letter that you wrote for my eighteenth birthday! These all belong to the steady flow of letters that I always get from you. Believe me, dear Ernst, whenever I write to you, I often think about how strange fate is—that you had to go so far away from here until we even got to know each other better and began saying "du" to each other!*

Ernst let Eddie Stritzel know about the woman in Germany that he cared about, something that Liselotte wasn't altogether comfortable with.

May 12, 1948

I think it's good that you have a friend. That means that you have someone that you can chat with and talk to about everything. It's too bad that he and his wife don't speak German, but then it's even better this way because you can learn more English. When I read that you've already told this man about me, I was a little surprised for a moment, but then I understood why you did that. But you really don't have to say too much about me. Otherwise, who knows what all of these people will think? And most of all, of course, you know the difficulties that need to be overcome until we see each other again, and then—I always needs to repeat this—I can only support you as a good friend from your home country, as I've done up to this point, and I also can't make a commitment, even after I've read all of your sweet letters. Many times I ask myself if you really understand that, but if you could put yourself in my position, dear Ernst, then you'd certainly understand it.

You know, I actually have a very serious temperament...

Before the middle of the year she also acceded to his request that she send him her picture. Even though she had a serious—even grave— expression in the photograph, it pleased him tremendously.

June 18. 1948

I've received another long, sweet letter from you, my dear Ernst. My deepest thanks, as always, for your words. And it was so very long; that's always wonderful. It makes me very happy to read that you like my picture and that it arrived safely. I know that I don't smile when I'm being photographed, but then, especially when amateur photographers are taking my picture during excursions, it's totally different. You know, I actually have a very serious temperament, but please —you don't have to imagine that I'm not able to laugh. I actually have a picture of myself in which I'm smiling, but I look pretty strange. In that case I actually had to start smiling fifteen minutes before the picture was taken, and when it actually was taken it wasn't a smile anymore, but instead a distorted expression that unfortunately doesn't look that good. But I'd already figured that it would turn out that way.

Around this time Liselotte began to assure him that, although she consorted with other men in Germany, she wasn't romantically involved with any of them. When she mentioned that someone walked her home after her evening English class, she stressed that she did this solely in the interest of safety.

Oct. 3, 1948

For quite a while now someone's been walking with me when I go home—but you also don't have to be concerned when I tell you that it's a man who comes along with me. He actually wants to emigrate to Pennsylvania, and he's already turned in his application forms; relatives of his are giving him financial help to do this. But he's really very gentlemanly and not like one of the others types you see today. Someone like that, of course, wouldn't attend classes. I think that someone's always walked with me since the start of 1947. Before this man it was someone who became a technical traffic superintendent in the German train system; he lives close to me. He didn't write the exam in January 1948, and so now he's not in my class. The man who now walks to my house with me was also already in my class. He didn't walk home with me before; that only started once our upper-division class had gotten a lot smaller. I hope that you understand this and don't misconstrue it. You know me, don't you?

When her classmate invited her to come to the *Wiese* with him, where the Munich Oktoberfest was in full swing, she turned him down and made sure that Ernst knew about her refusal.

Even though this man's invited me to go with him to the Wiese, I just didn't have time for that. But he's not pushy or fresh in any way at all. If he were like that, I wouldn't be the right person for him. For me it's a good thing because I don't have to take that route alone.

On October 24, 1948, Ernst tried his hand at poetry.

The following verses came to me during a lonely October evening that I spent thinking only about you. And so they're only meant for you, and today they'll begin their journey to you, my love.

Once I left my homeland—
That's nothing new anymore.
I wanted to see the world,
What was there to regret?

And so I went off to distance places.
I wanted to forget what once had been,
To begin again, to make a fresh start—
That's what my plan looked like.

Soon after that I was in New York,
A city that had everything
That I'd had to do without for so long.
I saw it all around me in abundance.

Then it really hit me for the first time,
That I'd started anew
In a strange country
With an empty sack.

And so now I stood in a new world
As a [in English] *greenhorn*
[in German] *Where the stuff of my dreams*
Soon mingled with things that troubled me.

Above all it was money
That gave me a headache
Because it was very hard to earn money
With poor English.

And now two years have gone by
Since I found a new beginning
In a land out West.
O God, thank you a thousand times.

But still, my thoughts often turn
Back to my homeland,
Munich and my mountains
Which I can never forget.

And something deep in my heart
That no one else knows about—
The love for a young woman,
The bond of friendship, and troubling times.

Never before had I felt
What love truly is,
Until love came to me
From far away and through my yearning.

You, cherished Liselotte,
At home in the Isar Valley,
All I still want here in [in English] *California*
[in German] *Is you.*

I ask you, my love,
6000 [in English] *miles* [in German] *away from here,*
Let our friendship flourish
Keep staying true to me!

His proclamations of love were just as open and expansive in a letter penned in the following month.

November 13, 1948

My dear Liselotte!

Today I really want to have another conversation with you, deal with all of the questions that we haven't touched on so far—and, besides that, I don't want to forget to thank you for a very sweet letter that you sent me.

Today—Saturday—I had to work again from seven to twelve, because at the moment we're swamped with work. During that time, of course, my thoughts turned to you a lot, and I decided to write to you this afternoon.

So, how are things going with you, my darling? You always write so affectionately to me that I can't thank you enough. You're so nice to me. When I think back on things, then I just can't wait until we're together once again.

I just have to kick myself. If I were just a little bit older, then I wouldn't have traveled so far away from you—but when I say that I'm assuming that I would have known then what I know today. But, as we already know, you can't get very far with the words "If it just had been…" The past just can't be changed, and so I have no choice but to use the present to hope for the future. As you always assure me, you're my loyal colleague; you should know that I always appreciate that. I just hope that at some point I'll really be able to offer and give you what you really wish and expect. I really love you so earnestly, and so I just hope that I can meet these challenges when I try to unite my fate with yours. Oh, dear Liselotte, please understand me—won't you?

I also often recall the experiences that we shared when we worked at the Reiner firm. I think that, in spite of everything, it was a nice time.

His protestations of affection continued unabated as 1949 got underway. In a letter dated January 30, 1949, he began with the words *My darling!* and took care to underscore that greeting three times.

Just a few quick greetings from my desk. The paper that I'm writing on is sitting on a large stack of work. It won't all get done this evening, because officially I've already ended my work for the day, and I want to write you before I head out to go home.

He ended with a touch of English—*So long!*—followed, in German, by one of his signature phrases—*Only your Ernest, the one that loves only you*—making sure to underline the final word a total of nine times.

Liselotte's rhetoric also suggested a greater sense of closeness and affection. Early in 1949 she wrapped up one of her letters this way:

My dear Ernst…I'll say "Good night" to you, and, as always, I'll take my leave by sending you the most affectionate greetings and my best wishes and I am, as always and in the future, merely [written in hand] *your Liselotte* [now typed again], *your friend in your homeland, who's loyal to you and who thinks about you very often. In spite of the great distance between us my thoughts are with you, and I await what fate has in store. Will it allow Ernst to come here some day?*

Goodbye, my darling!

He wanted her to write more frequently, and he didn't hesitate to let her know about this.

February 26, 1949

Dear Liselotte!

After eleven hours' worth of work I've finally come home so that I can write a few lines to my dear friend. But I'm honestly really tired—I've been haunted for a whole week now by a complicated stress analysis. I've often been working on it up to twelve hours every day, and I dream about it at night after I finally get to asleep. But the physical exhaustion that I'm experiencing at the moment doesn't even compare with the way I'm waiting for a sign of life from you. The whole week has gone by, and there hasn't been a letter.

Although the 1949 folder only contained a handful of full-length letters, it held a number of postcards that Liselotte had sent to Ernst during two road trips she undertook during that year.

In early June, for example, she sent him several postcards while traveling with her sister Käthe and Thomas, her nephew. The one dated June 11th showed a black-and-white photo of the graves of two authors, Ludwig Ganghofer and Ludwig Thoma, in Egern-Rottach, close to Tegernsee Lake. On the other side she formulated her thoughts entirely in English:

June 11, 1949

Dear Darling!

Little Thomas and I make just our walk before noon. Today it's cooler and there's a strong wind. Yesterday afternoon it was raining rather hard, so I couldn't leave the room. My sister had her birthday yesterday, and so we had a little party till night. I hope you can read my bad writing. Today it's very cloudy and no sunshine.

A June 12th card marked her visit to the Wallberg Chapel; in her June 14th card she described her trip to the Maria Eich Chapel. She probably had Ernst's devout Catholicism in mind when she selected these cards.

In October her travels took her the Zugspitze, the highest peak in Germany, as well as Lake Constance and Lucerne, Switzerland.

Her October 8, 1949 postcard hailed from the Swiss municipality of Einsiedeln.

Dear Ernst!

[in English] *Now I'm spending the first day in Switzerland.* [in German] *The trip here was just magnificent. Yesterday evening there was a grand light procession that lasted more than an hour going up and down the mountain. This morning there was a large ceremonial mass—complete with singing—in the church. I'll go into the details in my next letter. The weather's still beautiful. Today our trip will take us to Lake Lucerne…You are always in my thoughts…Many greetings, always yours—Liselotte*

At Thanksgiving Ernst let Liselotte know how grateful he was that she was such an abiding presence in his life.

November 24, 1949

<u>*My dear Liselotte!*</u>

Today I don't have to work, something that gave me a good chance to sleep in—and that did me a world of good. You know, today's a holiday in all of America—[in English] "Thanksgiving." *[in German] It's similar to a "Day of Thanks" in Germany, except that here it's traditionally celebrated with a turkey meal to honor the first [in English]* Thanksgiving *[in German]. But I don't want to leave you with the impression that, for me, the whole thing is just about eating—or what you would call "pigging out" in Munich-style German. No, definitely not—it's really a day that's devoted to giving thanks for everything that we have. And so I also want to take this sense of the holiday seriously, and especially on this day I want to be thankful for everything that could have so easily been very different and could have had a much darker outcome—but especially for the good fortune that I can still look forward to. I think that I can say this without hesitation, because having such a sweet girl as you, my friend—someone whom I met in such a strange and special way and who is so loyal to me—all of this is something that I definitely need to be thankful for. And so my thoughts are especially with you on this day, my darling in my old homeland, and even if no one around here knows about it, I'm particularly grateful for my loyal girl—not just today but always. I love you with all of my heart, and I'm looking forward so much to* the time when we can meet with each other and speak with each other again. But then, when we're together for always and we can celebrate Thanksgiving together, then we'll know that we've really earned that turkey. It's too bad that we'll still have to wait a while, and so in the meantime I'm glad that I can enjoy the words in your letters. I have a feeling that such a lovely letter will reach me tomorrow, and I just hope that I'm right.

Farewell until the next letter, and accept my warm and affectionate greetings, from your Ernst, who is always faithful to you.

Obviously we all use the casual form of address with each other...

During the 1950 Fasching season Liselotte continued to assuage any concerns that Ernst might have had about her lively social schedule, including her association with one Walter Gademann.

January 28, 1950

The grand ball will be held next Friday, February 3ʳᵈ, in the cafeteria of the technical college. There'll be a total of two hundred invited guests. That's always nice; everyone wants to go there, and above all it isn't that crowded. This will be my first Fasching ball this year. Everyone needs to be wearing a mask. Of course, it'll be a lot of fun when you can't recognize other people because of their masks. Once again the friends of W. G. will sit together at one table, and I've been invited to sit there as well...I have to say that it was really nice last year with the people from the technical university, because everyone behaved decently. Obviously we all use the casual form of address with each other—otherwise it wouldn't be a Fasching in Munich—but that custom only holds for that one evening. During that time using the formal address of "Sie" is forbidden. Besides, Fasching is a fun event—everyone knows that.

She landed upon an especially exotic choice for that year's Fasching costume.

You know, if you could see me in my costume, you'd laugh at the way that I look. You know who I'll be? I've chosen something that's very close to you—Hawaii! It was easy to make because I had the material from my mother, and so it was very cheap to put together. That's also very important… It's too dangerous to wear the thin chain on my wrist—it could break off and I could lose it—so I'll wear it around my ankle.

Just as Ernst had urged her to write more frequently, he also wanted more pictures of her—a lot more.

May 29, 1950

I especially want to thank you for your lovely picture. It's really very nice. Please be so kind as to send me a steady supply of such photos; then I'll be able to not just hear you "writing as I read," but I'll also be able to "see you on paper," as you grow ever lovelier.

When he wrote on June 4, 1950, to tell Liselotte at length about his surprise reunion with Peter Hold—a fellow inmate in Wolmirsleben—in San Francisco, he let her know that *During all of this I had to think a lot about you.*

From time to time he sent her postcards to keep her updated about his adventures in the Sierra Nevadas. The black-and-white photo on one of these, dated July 9, 1950, shows a large dead bear tied down to the top of a car. A sign below its head reads, "CAUGHT NEAR TAMARACK LODGE."

Dear Liselotte!

It's 11:30 PM, and we're on the way up to Ebetts Pass. I send you lots of love and affectionate greetings. As always, only

Yours Ernst

The Stritzels included their own greetings to her in the bottom left-hand corner: *Hello Eddie & Elsie.*

When Liselotte traveled to Berchtesgaden, a town close to a national park with the same name, she sent Ernst greetings of her own.

August 18, 1950

I'm now on vacation (unfortunately just for four days), something I let you know about in my last letter, and I send you the most affectionate greetings.

Today I was already in Berchtesgaden and in the salt mine. It was really very interesting and a lot of fun! The next time I'll tell you all about it. Most affectionately! Liselotte

She was taking this road trip with Hermann John, who signed his name beneath hers at the bottom of the card.

My dear girl, please don't be sad...

Out the blue another unexpected event happened, something that eventually precipitated the realization of Ernst's romantic dreams and hopes.

December 30, 1950

Please pull yourself together, my darling, because it's also not easy for me to share this with you. Well, last Thursday—two days ago—I received my induction order, and I'll have to report to the barracks on January 9, 1951. My job deferment came to an end in December, and so I'm now in line for this. My dear girl, please don't be sad, and don't believe that I won't be true to my promise in spite of everything. Who knows how fate will guide things, and it's possible that this means that we'll at least be able to see each other again, something we've yearned for so much. My mother is taking it especially hard because I have to go away, and then she'll be all alone. But there are countless young people who have been affected. I don't want to go into any more details about this today. Of course, now I've got a whole lot of things to do at work—to finish everything up, because I just don't want to drop everything. My boss is completely out of sorts because he's losing me, and he says that afterwards I should definitely come back to the same firm.

On the occasion of your birthday I wish you—my dear friend in my old homeland—all the best. I'm enclosing a small present and souvenir.

Liselotte shared the news with other people in Munich.

January 15, 1951

Everyone celebrated my birthday in a very nice way, and I'd like to thank you once more as well for your affectionate birthday wishes and your present, which I've been wearing since January 8ᵗʰ, 1951. It suits me well, and everyone says that the earrings look good on me. And so you see that you really did make a good choice. Mr. J. [John] is very sorry, by the way, that you've been called up for the military. You had so many plans and things to look forward to this year.

Liselotte received Ernst's first "soldier letter" in late January 1951, along with his new address. In her February 5, 1951 letter she regaled him with more stories about her Fasching exploits, probably to help him feel closer to his Bavarian origins.

Thanks so much for your birthday card and the other card from [Liselotte misspelled this] *Sakramento. Both of these got here on Friday. I also don't want to forget to thank you for the magazines that also came this week…I hope that my descriptions help you to imagine how things were at this year's Fasching season in Munich. I hope that you'll be able to breathe some of the "Fasching air" when I describe things!*

Ernst apparently sent her a picture of his own, one that his mother had taken.

February 9, 1951

Many thanks for your nice photo and your second letter from Fort Ord. The uniform looks good on you, but not having to wear a uniform would be more pleasant—don't you think so too? It's too bad that the picture is a little dark. I can see you for sure, but Mrs. Roesch somehow didn't capture the background all that well. You even have shiny buttons in the photo. What do these mean? Today marks the end of your first four weeks as a soldier! How many weeks or months will it be until you're allowed to return to your normal life? That's probably something that you don't know yourself—you know as little about that as I do, right?

The next part was underlined in blue ink, either by Ernst or Liselotte later on.

Can you apply for citizenship in spite of this? Would that even work out faster now, or how does that look?...Please give my regards to your mother when you see her again. I hope that it won't be so hard for her to be alone for a while. Everything will work out well; it won't last all that long! Will you be able to stay in the apartment—financially, I mean? That's certainly not everything that you need to pay for, and it's certainly not easy, because as a recruit you don't earn much money. Has the financial support for your mother been approved? That would be a small help at least, even if it isn't all that much, of course.

On the envelope she told him more about Fasching and then mentioned that she'd taken another road trip with Hermann John, this time to Lake Tegernsee in Upper Bavaria.

On Sunday the weather was very beautiful; that was when we drove to Rottach-Egern. It was very lovely.

Affectionately! Your Liselotte

Writing vertically along the side of the envelope, she concluded:

We shouldn't take everything so hard, my dear Ernst!

Your friend, Liselotte.

Liselotte falsely assumed that being a private was something special. Ernst was quick to set her straight.

March 10, 1951

The matter of "private" wasn't a promotion; it just had to do with a regulation which eliminates the rank of "recruit." But if you want to be proud of your "Ami-boyfriend" (and now that's really true in the actual sense of the word), then I'll share some news with you: I got the sharpshooter pin for my skills with an infantry rifle. I've only been in the military for two months now, and I've already gotten a decoration.

He completed his basic training at Fort Ord on Monterey Bay— far away from the mountains where he'd gone skiing with the Stritzels.

Here, on the coast of the Pacific Ocean, it's very cold a lot of the time, and two weeks ago we even got a little snow. Every time when I see the snow-covered cars going by, then (as someone in Munich would say) it "stinks and smokes" inside me.

In another letter written in March he let her know what some of his Army roommates were going through.

What you write is very true: "We can only hope; we can't make plans anymore." When I look around here, there are twenty-nine other soldiers in the same room with me. All of them are my age, and all of them have similar plans and hopes. Some are newly married, and for all us our plans—for a small house, a place to call home, and just what everyone wants to achieve— have been put on hold. We're still in training, but who knows where we'll be a short time from now? I'm just writing to this to show you that others are facing a situation that's like ours. Of course, in our case there are even more worries and difficulties. But it encourages me when I sometimes hear the comment: [in English, retaining his error] *"The first thing I'll do when I get out of this army is going home and marry my girl."*

Liselotte was often on his mind during those days and weeks.

April 4, 1951

<u>*My dear young woman!*</u> [Underlined twice]

Today I especially had to think a lot about you, and during instructional time I dreamed about all sorts of things with my eyes wide open. And so I decided to bring this day to a close by putting together some words for you.

How are you doing, my dear Liselotte? You know, I just can't help myself, and I keep brooding about everything, even though everything looks so gloomy. Isn't it peculiar, when you think about it, how complicated our situation has become?...

When we practice all sorts of things in our training, then I often think how beautiful and simple it would just be if the practice of warfare could just be discontinued. But even with all of the wisdom of the ages it just seems that this human race simply won't come to its senses and learn to value peace.

What's new in Munich, anyway? Please write me about different things when you have time so that I'm in the know about all of this.

I'm already looking forward to your next letter. With love and loyalty I remain, as always, only your Ernst.

When Ernst had the chance to visit his mother in Lodi, he found a package from Munich waiting for him there.

April 22, 1951

Dear Liselotte!

Last Thursday—I was on bivouac again for an entire week—your nice letter of the fourteenth of the month reached me. You definitely wouldn't have been able to recognize me—I was completely filthy and tired—and your letter was like a ray of sunlight. It was only late in the evening that I had the time to read your words in the tent by candlelight. And so for a short time my thoughts were solely with you…My joy was immense, and I'm very, very thankful for your words.

Yesterday evening at eight o'clock I arrived back here in Lodi, and my mother was beaming when she handed me your lovely birthday present. The ashtray is really wonderful, and it makes me really happy, and I'll also say "God bless you" with much affection for your gift…

During my time in the military many things have changed, of course, above all because all of my efforts (in my career and my work) to build and save for the future have been interrupted.

You asked about my car. Right now I'm considering whether I should sell it because its styling, if nothing else, will be so old by the time I can drive it again. What do you think about that? A lot depends on where my military duty will take me, because it's possible that I'll be able to bring it along with me.

During this time Liselotte maintained her close friendship with Hermann John, and she continued to be candid with Ernst about it. In a seven-page letter she detailed another extended trip that she and Hermann wanted to take.

April 22, 1951

Good morning, my dear Ernst!

Maybe it'll also be the evening when you get this letter, but you know, right now it's a bright spring morning where I am. The sun is shining…The sparrows in front of my window are almost drowning out the pretty chattering of the other birds with their screeching. Within the last two days the trees have become a lot greener…Both of the women who are with me are now going to church. But I'd rather write to you now, since I'm so totally alone up here and it's now the best time for me to write…At the very start of this letter I want to tell you about the trip that I'll be taking this coming week, from April 28th to May 5th, 1951, with Mr. John and, for part of the journey, also with his brother. Please understand me the right way, because I want to tell you about everything here—but I don't want to brag, and I don't want to hurt you.

She emphasized that her relationship with Hermann was platonic and would remain so.

No—I just wanted—and I want—that you also know about the wonderful trip that we want to take, and I want you to trust me, my dear Ernst. I think that I can say with certainty that even if I didn't know you, I'd be very standoffish because this is of course always the largest possession of a young woman, even if most people laugh about this "old-fashioned" point of view. Maybe you can't quite understand this sentence, but I can't express myself…

But now about the trip: We'll go along Lake Constance and this time we'll take the upper route (Überlingen, Radolfzell) to Sigmaringen. There Klaus John, his brother, will leave us. But we really want to keep going into the Black Forest area, which is supposed to be so magnificent. I hope that the weather will be good. Later on I'll tell you all about it. And so you won't get a letter from me this weekend; instead you'll definitely get a postcard with news—for sure!

My dear Ernst! I was very happy when I read "Lodi" in the return address section of your last letter…You were at home for your birthday… The main thing is that you could celebrate the day wonderfully. You mother was also happy, I'm sure. Were the Stritzels there as well? Have you heard anything from your firm in the meantime?

I figured something out from the information that you sent—that not everything is as hopeless and dark as it seems to me or to both of us right now. I just don't let myself be filled with great hopes that would then just be dashed—but it was pleasant to read that. My situation is just so complicated that I really like to hear something pleasant. Although things are going very well with me, I can't complain, because who around here has such a chance to travel in a car—the kind of opportunity that I've been offered? Of course, there are many here that can afford that, but only the people "up there," a group that I could never belong to. Over here everything's just too expensive— the gasoline taxes alone are so high. Where you are it's certainly better... Ernst, now I've got to interrupt my scribbling and set things up for breakfast; otherwise the two other women will be back and I won't be finished with that. I'll finish this up later!

Now I'm done, and I'll continue to write these lines to you. Unfortunately this letter will have to wait to be sent off until tomorrow, because I just found out that I don't have enough stamps for it anymore.

She still felt deeply conflicted about their prospects. Though she acknowledged that they might well marry in the future, she was also wary of committing to that dream completely due to the sheer length of their separation.

I earn a good salary and I can afford this and that. More than that, it's the fear that because this time of waiting has gone on for so long we've both changed. It's the fear that, when we do meet face-to-face at some point, we'll know each other because of our letters, for sure, but we'll actually be complete strangers outside of that. You know, dear Ernst, it might be that in this way I think a little too much...But I can't help myself. It's the truth—don't you think so too? You, of course, have a strong feeling that the two of us are connected. In one of your letters a while back you wrote to me that you'd never felt this feeling before...That's also very clear, because otherwise you wouldn't have tried so hard to get to know me better through letters and to meet with me personally as soon as possible. The man must, in my opinion, of course be completely convinced [about the relationship] *in advance. If the situation were reversed, the whole thing would be completely wrong...Then the same question pops up again and again: will we even have the opportunity at some point—if you're able to come over here—to get to know each other personally and thoroughly? Oh, these are a lot of questions that don't have answers—or what do you think?...*

My dear Ernst! I wish you all the best, and I hope that you understand what I've written today the right way. I send you lots of love and affectionate greetings. Your Liselotte [in English in the lower left-hand corner—misspelling retained] *Good bye!*

And then came the peripety that changed everything.

The content of this letter has certainly surprised you...

While Ernst's peers at Ford Ord were sent to Korea, he found himself reassigned to Berlin, where his facility with German would be of great value. From May 18th to May 29th he was transported to Europe aboard the USNS General Hodges.

Oddly enough, Ernst first contemplated catching Liselotte off-guard in Germany without even letting her know in advance that he'd be stationed in Berlin. Once en route, however, he changed his mind and put pen to paper.

Liselotte noted on the envelope of Ernst's May 1951 letter that he'd written it *"on the ship!"*

<u>*My dear Liselotte!*</u> [underlined twice]

It's been a long time since we've heard from each other—at least it seems that way. Maybe you were puzzled about what was happening all of a sudden. In the meantime this thread that connects our fate became tenuous, and maybe you were struck by that and worried about it.

Because I'm going over the great expanse of water and the water shows the moon's reflection, I'm thinking about so many things. My original plan was to surprise you with a visit—just to come to you one day unannounced. But somehow, I don't know why, I felt anxious; I asked myself whether that would actually be the right thing to do. And so I decided to write this letter. It's possible, of course, that we won't be that far away from each other for quite a while, but that we still won't be able to see each other. Please, my dear woman, understand the situation that I'm in and do your part so that we don't squander this reunion. Both of us have been waiting for this for so long. Both of us have been so concerned about it; we both believed that it would happen, and we've been looking forward to it for so long.

My dear young woman, I'm allowed to come to see you, right?...

I'll end this letter as Your Ernst, who is faithful to only you.

P.S. The content of this letter has certainly surprised you, and I wish that you could see you as you read it. But believe me—I'm so excited, and I'm anxiously looking forward to how things develop from this point.

Upon his arrival in Germany, he was sent to the 7720 Eucom Repl. Depot in Sonthofen/Allgäu, where he remained from May 30th to June 6th—and where Liselotte met with him for a five-hour visit on June 1st.

But just give me some time to get my bearings...

A few weeks later Ernst put together an eight-page letter reflecting on their rendezvous in Sonthofen. His words were permeated with his ongoing conviction that, somehow, they'd be able to overcome whatever obstacles still stood in their way.

June 17, 1951

My dear young woman!

Ever since I spoke with you the last time on the phone, I've been thinking about you even more than before. The way things have developed in general, of course, has had a significant effect. Isn't it peculiar? For several years everything about our situation was just a glimmer of hope which slowly got stronger, but suddenly it's shining now as if a dark cloud had covered its rays before. It wasn't easy for me, and it was a great agony for me. When I think about the way things were just a few months ago, I see very clearly how I felt back then. But like a miracle it suddenly become bright again. The anxiety turned into joyful excitement, and finally the day I longed for arrived—the day that for years had only been the image in a dream, the event that we'd never been able to arrange for. It was the first day of June, one that I'll never ever forget. How many times, when we were writing to each other, did we wish that we could at least see each other again one time? Yes, my darling, this wish, such a natural one, became a reality—in a modest way. We were able to meet; we could speak with each other; we were given five hours for our reunion. During this short time we spoke about all sorts of things. We told each other about things that had happened to us years ago. For me it was wonderful; I could hardly believe that I was together with my girl.

Ernst was somewhat uncomfortable and uncertain in her presence, and he tried to account for his conduct and explain his state of mind.

Then came the moment to say goodbye, and I had no idea how long that separation would last. I could have kissed you, and I wanted to kiss you to show my thankfulness, my joy, and my sadness. But—and I'll be very honest with you about this—I didn't dare do that. When all is said and done there was the chance that this separation would only last for a few days, that this first day of June would just signal the beginning of many times when we could get to know each other. Given the fact that I was actually with you, I trusted in this possibility. This is how I justified my behavior, because otherwise you might have thought badly about me. After all, there was the danger that everything that I'd been hoping for during the last few years—and that I'm still hoping for—would be ruined all at once. Do you understand me, my darling? It's possible that you're irritated about my not having kissed you, and maybe you're also irritated that I'm sharing my thoughts about this with you here.

Just as in his previous correspondence, Ernst placed great stock in being as open with Liselotte as he possibly could.

So far my letter has sounded like a confession, and in fact it is a confession. I'm not ashamed about that at all. Why shouldn't I show my true colors to the young woman that I intend to marry? No, I just think that if I act candidly and sincerely, then you'll have the chance to make a firm decision about something that really is the way it looks. I hope that you understand me the right way, my darling!...I know that I'm peculiar in many ways. Many people don't understand me, and they'll never have the chance to do so. It's just that I always take things in life harder than many other people do, but it's just like the proverb says: "A child who's been burned stays away from the fire."

Even though both now lived in what had been a single country, "Germany" was now a complex region, both politically and militarily.

Now I'm already in Berlin, so close and still so far from you. Once again there's a border that separates us, of course just to a limited degree. Once again I'll work hard so that we can meet again, even if it's just a short meeting. But just give me some time to get my bearings, and I'll figure something out and suggest another time that we can see each other. Let's just trust that God will continue to be with us, because we certainly agree that only guidance from above can bring us together—though that also means that we should make every effort we can to make this happen.

But this is what troubles me: tell me, my darling, isn't it a burden for you to be pulled into my life? It's definitely been a complicated life up until now. These sentences sound very harsh, but excuse me, because I can't find any milder words. Do you really trust in me, that all of the beautiful things that I've promised to you will truly come to pass?...You know about the things that we always wrote to each other—yes, you've also written about them enthusiastically. We'd even gone so far as to share ideas about how to decorate our apartment. As far as I'm concerned, these plans are still in place. We'll just have to start from further back because of my present situation, which has, so to speak, brought everything to a standstill—I'm talking about my financial situation. But I can still imagine that everything could turn out well and that it could all be accomplished if both of us are determined and if we stick together.

You might think that I take everything so hard and that I don't even know what's what anymore. If I just had some good advice from someone. Please be so kind and at least write to me often. But please, just write about the two of us.

He closed by soliciting her thoughts about how they might now proceed.

My darling, please write to me soon, and write often. Maybe you've got some suggestions about what to do now...I wish for and hope that I'm allowed to see you now and then. (That really can't be asking for too much.)

Early in his July 1, 1951 letter Ernst compared their developing friendship to a multivolume work of literature.

<u>*My dear Liselotte!*</u> [underlined twice]

I'm overjoyed that our correspondence has started up again...

The second volume of our book, so to speak, has begun with your June 25th letter. The first volume ended in a suspenseful way. Let's hope that the second volume doesn't just bring clarity and a conclusion, but that it's also followed by an authentic "book of life" that contains neither ink nor paper. Because life is also like a book: every day is a new page that, once written down, can't be erased anymore. We never know what the next page will bring with it, but we can use the previous pages—that is, we can use them by evaluating our previous experiences.

You certainly wrote very sincerely, and—to be quite honest—what you wrote freed me from a lot of uncertainty and pensiveness. Unfortunately, it wasn't possible for me to begin corresponding with you again sooner, and this in itself was already a burden for me—one that can't be underestimated— because constantly wondering when and how I'd be able to send you letters again definitely had to do with some complicated circumstances.

I'm glad that, when you returned to Munich, you wanted us to get to know each other better. This is just about the most auspicious thing that I can honestly give myself credit for—even though I tend to exaggerate. Just imagine my situation. Couldn't someone just say: "That man is really hoping for 'slow but sure'?" Oh well – to stop joking around—but it's true, isn't it? Yes, of course I can understand what you wrote, but I'm not really satisfied. But I'd like to add that I've learned to be understanding about many things. It's a quality that many people very much respect me for, but it's also meant that many times I've gotten the short end of the stick.

At times he sized up postwar Berlin as he was now experiencing it.

July 7, 1951

Berlin—it's the first time that I've been in this city. Until now I haven't been able to decide whether the natives here would prefer hearing Bavarian German or English—that is, which foreigner they like less.

He seasoned the next section with Bavarian spelling and idioms.

They really don't have much affection for the Bavarians—I've figured that out.

He was now an outsider at least two ways—an American soldier in Germany, and a Bavarian at heart stationed in the midst of Prussians. One afternoon he was drinking coffee at the Hotel Stadt Wien along the Kurfürstendamm, one of Berlin's major boulevards, when he was drawn into a conversation with two of the locals.

Two elderly ladies who sat at the same table asked me about the program at the Berlin Opera House. I tried to speak in my very best High German, and I got complimented about how perfectly I could talk that way. They *wound up telling me that I didn't have an American accent, but rather a Bavarian one. "Oh," I said, "I guess I acquired that. I was stationed in Upper Bavaria for a while." I <u>didn't</u> lie, did I?*

Now, my darling, I'd better wrap this letter up on this sheet of paper. I hope that you're somewhat interested in my remarks. Maybe they'll help you to understand me better, and they'll serve as a small window into the future that I want to offer you.

Waiting impatiently for your next letter, I'll say "Good Night" for today.

In August they both began to plan an extended reunion, something far more substantial and meaningful than just a five-hour rendezvous. In his August 3, 1951 letter Ernst wanted her to make sure that *nothing interferes between the fifteen and thirtieth of September—then my trip to you should be able to take place. My vacation time will presumably be ten days long.*

When Ernst spoke with his commanding officer about getting travel documents for this period, their talk took an unexpected turn.

Just imagine what I was asked at that time: [in English] *"Are you sure that she didn't run around with other G.I.'s while you were away?" "I'm sure she didn't, sir!"* [in German] *was my answer – and I didn't have to think about it before telling him that. I said the truth, didn't I? (Now I've said the wrong thing, and if I keep this up then you'll probably decide that I shouldn't come to you at all.) No, I just gave myself permission to make a small joke, and my superior officer certainly just wanted to irritate me with this almost insulting comment.*

Getting married would be possible three months before I leave the military...

Within the next few days Ernst put together several other letters. In one of them he burned the midnight oil as he described the vacation that he had in mind as well as a grander, more long-range game plan for their future.

August 10, 1951

<u>*My dear young woman!*</u> [underlined twice]

I want to respond to your letter of the sixth of the month right away so that we can avoid any unnecessary delay in our correspondence.

Here are some additions to what I've told you about so far; they're about something that we're both interested in:

a)   *The Vacation That We're Planning:*

We're permitted to go to all American recreation sites such as clubs, restaurants, performances, and similar places. I'm the only one who can stay in American accommodations (hotels and places like that) because we're not married. Of course, I'd have to make a reservation in advance to do this. On the other hand, I was right to think that I can make use of all German establishments, including hotels. We're certainly better off being as flexible as possible when we make our plans—so we should be able to change every plan we've made, and so I think it's advantageous to use German marks when we pay for accommodations as much as possible, and I'm sure that we'll find places to stay. In the worst case we could stay in a mountain cabin.

Oftentimes Liselotte had cautioned Ernst about making detailed plans, but here he ignored such counsel, delineating his vision of the coming years as he imagined they could unfold.

b)   *Our Extended Five-Year Plan:*

This seems to have been extended to six years. At any rate, if I'm discharged next year, it's possible that we can go over to America together, once we've gotten married before then. Getting married would be possible three months before I leave the military, but the application has to be submitted nine months before then. The American government requires six hundred dollars from me for that, and naturally we'll get half of that back after you've been in the U.S.A. for three months. This is, so to say, supposed to be for your benefit, in case you want to give up everything within three months and go back to Europe—so it's three hundred dollars for travel money that the United

States government has set aside. *I'm only writing this because I assume that you're interested in why this whole procedure is set up this way. I know, of course, that you'll never make use of this; that's why I wrote, of course, that* <u>we</u> *will get three hundred dollars back.*

On several occasions in his Berlin letters Ernst alluded to "Elizabeth," a popular radio song in which the singer apparently asks a woman to marry him and anxiously hopes for her consent.

So much for these bits of news. But once again I have to think about "Elizabeth," that hit song. Tell me, why do you make it so difficult for me? Now once again you're starting to let me know that you also have your quirks as well, and that you might not match my expectations. But just be smart. You don't want to advise me against this. For me to give up now is out of the question. You just want to irritate me a little, and I get that, but a joke like that one won't undermine my resolve by a long shot.

If expressed as a humorous story, it would look like this: For five long years a young man pursues a beautiful young woman. Whether the ground is also moving in the other direction or she's running away from him isn't clear at the moment. While he's running, he passes by all of the other young women without even noticing them. (No, sometimes he does look here and there, but he's definitely never stood still.) He concentrates only on the woman in front of him. He only approaches her slowly, but he notices that as this happens her heart starts to beat more anxiously. Things get better and worse for him, but he doesn't get winded. All of a sudden she turns around and says: "Just look at me for once and consider whether you're really running after the right one!" But he doesn't take any time for this at all. Instead he runs on toward her—that is, rather than going back, he accepts the risk that at some point he might be brought back in an ambulance.

Now you wanted to know why I told my commanding officers how things really are. Why should I have lied? Is what we're planning something illegal?

So, my darling, let's go forward and have a successful vacation.

In the meantime the eleventh of August has started, and I can't mail this letter until Monday.

Perhaps because he had Liselotte's road trips with Hermann John in mind, he lowered her expectations about some aspects of their own travel arrangements.

I hope that you're really looking forward to our vacation as much as I am. In the terms of travel experiences it's very possible that it won't be as great as you expected...It's easily possible that you already have nicer vacations to look back on, because we don't have car transportation and things like that at our disposal, unfortunately. But don't you also think that this time around it's less important to tour a part of the world, but rather for us to get to know each other better? In this sense it could be the most beautiful experience up to now for both of us. Don't you think so too? Yes, and if both of us think that we're a little peculiar, then we'll just have to try to balance that out. Of course, that's only possible if we have the determination and wish to do so.

Until we see each other again, keep behaving yourself, and if you really like your friend, then overlook the fact that he's now branded as an "Ami."

Liselotte took an active role in making their vacation plans.

August 14, 1951

<u>My dear Liselotte!</u> [Underlined twice]

I've just gotten back from night school, and I want to write a quick answer to your letter of August 8th.

So far I really like all of your suggestions for vacation. I hope that you were able to get the accommodations for about four or five days in Bad Reichenhall—I mean, two rooms. Unfortunately, I can't give you an exact date in advance. That's why I wrote that we need to be flexible when we make our plans. Even the date of my arrival in Munich could shift by as many as three days. This is what I mean: let's assume that I'm allowed to leave here on Friday night. If I can fly in a military plane, then I'll soon be with you—unless the plane travels by way of Frankfurt and the layover in Frankfurt takes a long time. [in English] *Civil* [in German] *airplanes don't fly on Sunday; on other days they only fly once per day. But let's wait and see. Maybe I'll find out the exact day during the next three weeks. Finding accommodations in Munich is the least of my concerns. I'll write to some old neighbors, a school friend of mine; I'll definitely be able to stay there. You know, the people are very good acquaintances, and they'd possibly be offended if I stayed in a hotel. But this also could be taken care of, especially if we go away right after my arrival (one day later) so practically no one will know that I was in Munich. You know, I'll have make some formal calls on various people as a favor to my mother.*

Ernst stressed that he wanted to keep these other social obligations to a minimum.

August 15, 1951

So, as I've already told you, during this next vacation I'm mainly concerned that we get to know and understand each other better. That means that I'll only make the most necessary visits in Munich that I need to for my mother; I can take care of that in two days…Beyond that, I'd like to get to know your parents, speak with Miss Reiner and Doctor Gademan, and visit my father's grave. You surely understand that. Of course, you can come along with me for all of this if you want. But, as I've already said, I'm not embarrassed to say that this time around I want to be selfish—that is, I want to concentrate on my own concerns, which means that I finally want to convince myself completely that we'll be together in the future.

By the way, you wrote something in the letter before this most recent one: "<u>Yes</u>, it's impossible in one week." Don't you also believe that right now you can't say at all how you'll feel after this week? We can't change fate and the time that we've been called to live in, <u>but</u> we can try to adjust to the circumstances. We must, <u>unfortunately</u>, be realists rather than idealists. By the way, this also applies to many other people in this era.

Once again he seemed to be sending off more letters to Liselotte than he was getting from her.

August 23, 1951

<u>*My dear young woman,*</u>

Every day I've postponed writing letters, and I told myself that something has to be coming from you soon. It was only today that it finally happened. Your letter of the eighteenth of the month has arrived here. Even though I had to wait a long time for it, I was still—as always up to now—very happy and thankful about what you wrote.

Liselotte felt growing pressure about the coming days, and Ernst addressed her concerns head-on.

You know, sometimes I wonder if I can really know how things look inside the heart of a young woman who's been tested in such a rough way... But can you imagine how it might look inside me? Well, my darling, I think that both of us are making things more difficult than they really are. Instead we should let everything take its natural course. Of course we should also take action, using our reason. Seeing this situation fatalistically would also be wrong, because as individuals we have a free will that gives us, to some extent, the chance to shape our future according to our feelings. And so, my darling, in this sense I'll try to honor your wish that I have understanding for you. Anyway, don't be anxious, but rather look forward to our upcoming vacation joyfully instead of with fear that you might have make a difficult decision.

Here are some details. I'll try to get away from here on a weekend, on Friday or Saturday, and maybe I'll fly on Air France. That way—even though it's more expensive—I'd save a whole lot of time...I'm glad that you also prefer to use German accommodations, and I hope that you won't be embarrassed with me. I'll let you know later on about how and where we'll spend the night in Munich. I still haven't heard from my friend in Schwabing [a borough in Munich]*, and I only wrote to him recently. Anyway it'd be ridiculous if I couldn't find a place to stay in my old home town. But it's very nice of you that you're thinking about everything, and I hope that you're lucky with the reservations in Bad Reichenhall. Of course, you don't have to let on that the person traveling with you is a soldier; they'll notice that on their own...Let the people be surprised—why should we be concerned about that?*

You know, it all depends on reciprocity...

In a handwritten note on August 25, 1951, he shared the details of his finalized travel arrangements.

My dear young woman! [underlined twice]

I hope that you're not irritated with me because I "cooked up" my last letter to you at the typewriter.

So here, once again, are some details about our vacation...

Departure on Air France: Berlin, September 14, 1951, 16.35 PM
Arrival: Munich-Riem, September 14, 1951, 19.05 PM
Departure from Munich to Berlin: September 24, 1951, 7:45 AM

And so I'll arrive in Munich to see you on a Friday evening—at the start of a weekend, as you wanted. I've passed on the information that was given to me, but I can't say for sure that a change (on my end, naturally) is out of the question. But I'm sure that you're also happy to have a general idea about the times.

So, my darling, in three weeks we'll be together again. That will be great, won't it? Are you also looking forward to it already? What could you do about reservations in Reichenhall, etc.? As I've already said, I'm leaving the actual vacation schedule up to you, but you'll certainly let me put in my two cents when it comes to organizing our travel program. Anyway I wouldn't want to leave Munich any later than Monday morning (September 17th) so that we start our vacation trip as soon as possible.

He signed his name as *Ernstl* rather than Ernst here, a chummy variant of his Christian name.

In June and July 1988 Käthe and Walter Baumgärtner, our mother's sister and brother-in-law, flew over to California and visited with us in Lodi for a few days. After that they and our parents left for a meticulously planned trip to some national parks. A three-ring binder contains all of our father's comprehensive preparations for that tour—including a precise drawing of how everyone's luggage was to be arranged in the trunk of the family car.

Ernst's proposals for his 1951 vacation with Liselotte, drawn up in Berlin, betrayed the same scrupulous attention to detail. For example, on August 27, 1951, he let her know that *I'm already totally excited, and I just hope that everything will work out well and that the time before vacation goes by fast—and that the actual vacation moves by relatively slowly. I just hope that you still get something for us in Reichenhall. Make a deposit if that's necessary, and I'll pay you back later on.*

I like your suggestion that the first Saturday should be used to take care of private matters. Half of Friday evening will be taken up, of course, by getting settled in our accommodations, but this way I'll also have visited my friend and his mother, something that I have to do. *Saturday evening* [in English, including Ernst's error:] *May I have a date with you? Would you make reservations for the opera house etc. or wherever you'd like to go. If you want to, the 15th of September is going to be our first big date.* [in German] *I really like the idea of visiting your parents on Sunday, and I'm really looking forward to that. I hope that it's a pleasant visit, that I'm not tongue-tied and that your parents won't be disappointed. You know, you'll have to help me out a little—please! On Sunday evening we'll have to retire early, and on Monday morning—very early in the morning—we'll hit the road. Yes, and then I'll be in your power—me, the poor Ami!*

You do understand my joke, don't you? Because you can certainly sense just how much I'm looking forward to this. You know, I just wanted to pay you back with my comment, because again and again you've stressed that you want to have a vacation, rest, and relaxation—as if it could even be anything different with me along. By the way, do people work on Saturday in the Reiner firm? If that's the case, then maybe we could look by the firm on Saturday morning…

Of course, these are all just suggestions, and I'm fine with any changes that you want to make.

You know, quite honestly, I think that these three months in Berlin have helped me get used to life in Germany once again, at least to some degree. Because you have to admit that I was completely alienated by many things in Sonthofen. I wasn't even sure how to order in a restaurant here, etc. Since then I've had more practice with things like that, even when it comes to speaking in German. You claimed that I had an American accent; hopefully I haven't traded that in for a Berlin accent now. Sometimes I just have to laugh about myself, because I had a completely false impression about many things in postwar Germany. Since then, however, I know that poverty no longer exists here the way that it used to five years ago. Yes, many people here who have experienced how things have gradually improved don't remember those earlier times as well as I do. The contents of my packages to you from the U.S.A. will maybe show you how ignorant I was, but you doubtless didn't want to hurt my feelings and tell me that I often sent you something silly!

And so you ask me again and again not to exaggerate anything when we're on vacation. On the contrary, I'm afraid that I don't have the guts to do anything that even comes close to that. And so I also want to ask you not to make it too hard for me, but rather to stand by me and to help me to understand you, and to convince me that for five long years I was actually putting my faith in something that was real. You know, it all depends on reciprocity…I really believe that after a few days alone with you I'll be able to judge whether what I am and what I can offer you actually corresponds to what you want in the future, because I won't hesitate to share everything good and also everything harsh with you. Naturally, I need your understanding for this. I need you to work with me by offering criticism and wanting to understand at the same time. And so your interest, not just mine, is necessary so that a decision can be reached. So please don't think that it's impossible, because if it's the biggest decision in our lives and it touches on higher things and not just worldly things, then it's just a fact that everything that's accomplished in this world is something someone else thought was impossible.

Liselotte was excited to hear that he'd gotten a promotion in the military.

September 1, 1951

Many thanks for your congratulations about the PFC ["Private First Class"]. *It's still nice for me to know that military titles impress you, because I also don't think all that much about them, except for the extra nine dollars that I can now spend. It's a ridiculous pay raise; it means about five hours of work at my job—but even so it's equal to 36.20 German marks.*

Please, please tell me about it.

As the days of their vacation drew ever closer, Ernst's agitation grew.

September 4, 1951

You know, I'm already totally excited about the coming vacation, and my boss says that he hopes that I'll feel better when I return. Well, in the meantime everything has been finalized, and I'll arrive in Munich-Riem on September 14th at 19:05. When I have some time to get away tomorrow, I'll get the reservation and plane ticket right away at Air France. Now I'm just waiting for the [in English] *"Travelling Order"...*

Despite his best efforts Ernst's typewritten letters continued to be riddled with corrected errors and the occasional overlooked typo.

September 1, 1951

My dear young woman,

Today your sweet letter of the twenty-eighth of the month arrived. The last time I apologized because of the typing; today I'm perpetrating the same misdeed once again. But you're the one who's to blame for this. If you hadn't praised me so much, then it wouldn't have gone to my head. But for your information—and so that you (as a secretary who works in an office) also have something to laugh about—I'll let you know that I'm typing this masterpiece as an amateur—with two fingers...

But now to write about our vacation again...Well, I'm really happy that things worked out with the rooms. I think that the price is fantastic. How could you find something that was so cheap? If I'd arranged for the rooms when I was dressed in my uniform, they would have definitely raised the price right away. You—do you really think that I need to buy a winter coat? You know, our coats are such a bother—even if they're warm—and I think I should just take along my field jacket (the gray windbreaker) and hope that this matches the [in English] *Munich Military Post's* [in German] *uniform regulations.*

As soon as I have more details, I'll write you about them right away.

I'm already looking forward so much to this short time that we have at our disposal. But above all I'm looking forward to you, and I hope that you'll understand me—that I'm allowed to speak sincerely to a person—and I hope that you'll also have trust, even though I'm certainly, given my quirks, not flawless. But that should be my goal: not just to show my positive features, but to act naturally when I'm with you so that you can get a genuine sense of who I am. This might not be the wisest way to act around one's future bride, but it's the only right thing to do to remove, in advance, disappointments that might arise later on. You'll have to admit that I've always acted like this my letters from California. Naturally this assumes an extraordinary amount of understanding on your part, something that I've always asked of you, and I hope that you won't disappoint me, especially now. But, no matter how things turn out, I want to ask you for one thing:

If I don't please you in some ways; if you find out that you've made a mistake about the sort of person that I am; if something about the shared future that I'm promising for us doesn't match what you want; then please, please tell me about it. Don't be "considerate" or feel sorry for me. (I think that especially someone like you might do the latter.) Instead be totally honest, even if your words are harsh. You can believe that this section in particular wasn't easy for me to write, and I can certainly assume that another man probably wouldn't speak this way with you. You know that I really like you a lot, that I treasure you more than any other woman in the world...I hope that you'll really understand me as well as I wish you will.

You know, my darling, this world that we were chosen for is actually a very dirty place. You'd have to ignore what you see to think differently...These observations have long led me to look at my wasted youth as something that wasn't even that unusual. That's why my aim is to be successful and honest in the circumstances I have—and happy because I am this way—but not to squeeze out the best from the worst of this era and to be recklessly happy this way. That's something that I see every day, something that makes me angry inside, and, along with other things, it's why I call this world a dirty one.

I don't know why I always write about such things now and then—whether these sorts of discussions interest you at all. But this topic is connected with true love, at least for me.

"Love," I say. Certainly there are also ridiculous explanations, and a ridiculous number of explanations. It's peculiar what some people think love is. Sometimes I think to myself that everyone's right and only I have the wrong idea. But that's also totally unimportant. What's crucial for the two of us is that we both have the same sense of what it means to be happy. What I want for you and me is that, during this first chance for us to discover more about each other, we succeed in doing just that.

On the same day Ernst generated a second letter.

A week from now we'll be together again. Are you looking forward to it? You know, I can't even get much sleep, and it's especially tough for me to fall asleep because I'm brooding so much and making so many plans.

Now I've already got my plane ticket in my pocket, and so I'm just still waiting for the U.S. travel documents. I heard some news in the meantime from my friend and his mother—you'll definitely have to meet her. They've invited me to live with them while I'm in Munich. Well then, my darling— until 7:15 in the evening in Munich-Riem!

I'm already anxious to see how things look in Munich now. But on Friday I'll still have to steer clear of the street so that the military police don't catch me, because my vacation doesn't actually begin until Saturday.

In postwar Germany, our mother told us, it was frowned upon when German women were seen fraternizing with American soldiers. Liselotte was anxious about how her trip with Ernst would appear to others, whereas Ernst—given his Bavarian origins—didn't share her concerns.

September 4, 1951

But I can't understand why you don't want to be seen with me when I'm wearing my uniform. If you meet an acquaintance, then you can just simply introduce me. Then the people will see that I speak Bavarian German, and later on you can explain that your Ami is a friend from your youth who emigrated to America and who's now here once again to visit you. That's really nothing wrong or scandalous. It fits the facts, and it's a part of our actual history, something that can be explained in full later on without any guilty conscience. The same is true for my visit to Telefon-Reiner. I'll say the truth— that I'm traveling—and I'll keep the details to myself, details that Dr. G. and Miss Reiner certainly know about already. I'd never lie to Miss Reiner, and I can keep the other details to myself when I'm speaking with the others, or be ambiguous as a last resort. So, you see, it's not that hard to be honest!

Ernst wanted to take advantage of his time in Munich to check into the possibility of getting a position there—closer to Liselotte.

You already know that I'm trying to get a transfer, and it'd be worth sacrificing one day to take care of that. It's possible that Doctor G. knows someone there.

We'll go out to eat, of course, if you'll be kind enough to pick me up. Then we'll be able to talk about everything, and we'll see how everything goes from that time on…

One more question: If you spend the night in a hotel as a German, do you have to show your papers? Is there a danger that people ask to see your papers when you're on the street or in restaurants? You certainly know what I'm thinking about, and please be diplomatic when you answer; maybe I'll take that risk because of you.

He also wanted, understandably, to go to the Forest Cemetery.

I'm happy that you want to visit my father's grave with me. As a favor to my mother I've got to go there and also to my grandmother's grave, but it's closed there on Saturday and it might be that we'll have to go there on Sunday morning. By the way, you won't be able to sleep in late, because you'll be attending church with me on Sunday morning. We owe our Lord God that much, for sure. Thank you for saying yes for our date on Saturday. Well, we won't be getting much sleep over vacation. Time in the office is meant for that, not vacation!

I hope that this time that we've been allowed to share will help us to get to know each other better, and that it'll help both of us.

I just wish that I could tell you exactly how I feel at this moment…

September 14th finally arrived, and intention was transmuted into reality. Ernst boarded an Air France plane, flew from Berlin to Munich, and their much anticipated and meticulously planned reunion took place at long last. The two could spend some time together in Munich and then subsequently went on a tour that took them to Bad Reichenhall, Berchtesgaden, and Salzburg. All the highlights of these days were later carefully and lovingly documented in a beet-red photo album, and affixed inside its front cover was a card that bore a German poem in bold Gothic print:

To know someone
who understands you completely,
who always has your back in times
of trouble—who also loves your
shortcomings
because you belong to him—
then everything can break apart—
You'll never be alone!

Surrounding the poem at twelve, five, and seven o'clock were three small black-and-white pictures. Two featured my parents as a young couple, and the third showed my father alone on the ship en route to Europe, a cigarette jammed into his mouth, his eyes meeting the camera with a resolute, no-nonsense squint.

Judging from the album, their reunion got underway with a low-key stroll through central Munich, a bit of sightseeing, and a gathering and celebration of memories.

They went to Bad Reichenhall on September 17th and toured the spa garden there on the 18th, Ernst always clad in his U.S. Army uniform.

One picture in the album shows Liselotte standing in front of a wall; behind her gigantic graffiti letters proclaim "AMI GO HOME." Below that photo, using her stenographic writing, Liselotte asked, "What's this supposed to mean? Do these words apply to me?" Acting as Ernst's pen pal was one thing, but associating with him in public places put her at odds with many other Germans.

September 19th found them in Berchtesgaden as well as Obersalberg. One photo, snapped at a Berchtesgaden "Recreation Area," shows two Volkswagens parked side by side in front of a storefront. Noteworthy is that all of the signs in and above the display windows are in English—"Hunting," "Fishing," and "Information," and "Tours," among others.

On the 19th they also took in Hintersee Lake; on the following day they saw two other lakes, the Königsee as well as the Obersee.

During their time in Salzburg on September 27th they viewed the castle, the Mozart monument, and the cathedral.

The pictures usually show them in picturesque settings—along the shore of a mountain lake, or seated close to a hiking path next to a scenic meadow—looking posed and poised, but also glowing with genuine happiness. These locations presaged the hikes they'd enjoy taking years later in Yosemite and elsewhere.

For Ernst, this span of days was in a very real sense a dream of his that had come true.

He flew back to Berlin late on the 24th, and the next day he let Liselotte know how much he had cherished their time together.

September 25, 1951

<u>*My dear Liselotte!*</u> [underlined twice]

It's seventy-thirty in the evening, and I just wish that I could tell you on paper exactly how I feel at this moment. We said goodbye to each other nineteen hours ago. Today I got here at five minutes after ten, and when my co-workers greeted me they saw a completely changed man. I'd gained a little weight, I was in a much better mood—and people told me all sorts of other things as well.

Yes, I also think that I was still full of bliss at that point, even though I really felt sad on the plane. But in the meantime I've changed back again somehow, and if I'd written this letter right away this morning, it would definitely look different. I got into the taxi at eighteen minutes after midnight, meaning that I'd been with you up to a few seconds before then. Now it seems to me that I've lost everything, as if I've left behind what I value above all else. Somehow I'm filled with a vast fear, as if something might slam into me, and as soon as I finish writing this letter I'll go to bed and try to calm this fear with the solace of sleep.

On at least one occasion Liselotte had spoken bluntly with him about his longstanding hopes and convictions.

Now I have to think about what you said yesterday evening, when we were sitting in that nice restaurant. Now I know why you were disappointed in the way I was—that is, why you doubted my maturity. Beyond that I now know why I became aware in Bad Reichenhall that this was the most beautiful week of my life up to this point—something that I also told you, because I had the most incredible sense of inner peace that I'd ever felt. Please don't make fun of me, my darling, but rather believe that your presence definitely made me change in a profound way. Oh, if I could just always have you with me!

It could be that this letter, something that I'm writing just a few hours after our reunion, doesn't sound like the Ernst that you saw during vacation. But I can't act any other way, dear Liselotte, and I'll keep on writing this way to you, the way I feel inside in these moments. I trust that you'll understand my situation. I feel that I need you, and I hope that isn't a burden for you.

On occasion Liselotte's fears about being seen with an American had proved to be all too prescient.

And now I still want to say "Thank you" for your patience and your kindness during our (and my) lovely vacation—as well for your sacrifice… when you became the target of some people's harassing gestures and comments.

I'm already looking forward to your next letter, and I'm especially hoping that you'll soon confirm what I so firmly and sincerely believe, and I hope that we can see each other again soon.

With sincere love
always only your Ernst.

They were engaged in early November. Their two official engagement photos, timed to be shared with others at Christmas in 1951, make for a striking contrast. In one picture both are side by side, grinning at the camera.

In the other Liselotte is seated in an armchair, while Ernst is posed to her left behind her, maybe seated on a table. Here both are in a far more reflective mood, and Ernst's expression—one of profound joy and serenity—is especially telling.

People would say that we are in love!

Their journey from engagement to the wedding in October 1952 was riddled with bureaucratic hurdles and informed by ongoing practical considerations about how to orchestrate their lives in California.

Just as they'd collaborated on plans for their vacation in 1951, they now began exchanging thoughts about how their monthly budget in Lodi should be structured. For her part, in an undated letter from 1952, Liselotte counselled financial prudence. She also acknowledged the difficulty of devising plans for a life in the States while she still lived so far away from her future home.

I've read over your financial plan very carefully, but unfortunately I can't make a firm decision yet. On one hand, setting aside seventy-five dollars and saving up for a house is a very tempting idea; on the other hand, we shouldn't stick to this approach no matter what and then not be able to save anything else or much else, because a rainy day fund is more important over there than here…It also wouldn't be very nice for us to set aside money conscientiously for a house and at the same time not dare spend money on a vacation or something like that. But please, dear Ernst, these are just my thoughts, and so this doesn't constitute a decision, because that's something that I could never do. Maybe we can talk about this again; we could even do this when we're over there. Then we'll also see what's specifically available—I mean, what sort of an apartment we can find, or maybe a reasonably priced house that you think we should grab right away. From over here it's not so simple to figure out things like that.

On January 30, 1952, Ernst got another official travel authorization, one which gave him a seventy-two-hour pass to go to Munich on February 2nd. As his handwritten note on the form shows, he went by train this time, going overnight from Berlin to Munich, changing trains at Frankfurt, and returning along the same route.

Ernst prepared the section of the 1952 photo album devoted to this reunion, as his precise all-capitals writing makes plain. Here nearly all of his page titles, as well as the captions for individual photographs and additional comments, are in English.

On February 2nd, for example, he and Liselotte attended the WEISSEN RÖSSEL BALL IN MUNICH. As far as I can tell, this was his initial Fasching experience, his initiation into these colorful Munich traditions. Liselotte, by contrast, was now an old hand, an adept veteran in such matters. This first Fasching event was quickly followed by others, including one ball in the German Theater on the same evening. That year Liselotte sported a whole spectrum of Fasching costumes, including a Hawaiian girl, a Columbine, a Venetian woman, and something new—an "American girl" with rolled-up jeans and a flowery short-sleeved blouse.

Ernst got leave to travel to Munich at Easter in 1952, and he and Liselotte visited with her parents. The pictures make it plain that he'd already established an amiable rapport with both of them.

Around Easter he and Liselotte also traveled to Wallberg and Tegernsee. Once again the photographs in the album are often accompanied with captions in English. One page includes two pictures, one of each of them standing at a picturesque vista point. Both are looking at the camera with uncompromising seriousness. Ernst's caption takes the form of a dialogue:

Question: Why no smile?

Answer: People would say that we are in love!

Ernst later comments that on Easter Sunday they took *A wonderful walk which we'll never forget!!!!!!* and that *I was waiting for this moment since 1949.*

In the second half of June Ernst received yet another travel authorization, this time for ten days, and he and Liselotte used that time to travel to Switzerland, checking out St. Moritz and Pontresina, St. Gottherd Pass, and Zermatt. The typed, two-page itinerary that Ernst prepared and sent to Liselotte care of her work address in Munich lists the precise times of all of their train connections. Comments to the right of these times address the activities they'll engage in at each stop—museums, motorboat rides—as well as important reminders. Ernst warns Liselotte here, for example, that on June 28th they'll have to arrive the Grindelwald train station in plenty of time for their 8:33 AM train; that way they'll definitely get good seats.

Some faded flowers are stapled to the Palü Glacier page.

Ernst's two-day travel papers in August allowed him to visit Liselotte briefly in Munich.

This time he donned civilian clothes as he and Liselotte strolled down Leopold Street and later viewed the New Town Hall with her.

Well, today I wanted to hand in our papers…

Arranging to get married and then travel to America involved a mountain of paperwork. This was partly because Ernst was an American soldier, while Liselotte was German. Another factor was the distance between them. Ernst was now back in Berlin, while Liselotte still lived in Bavaria, meaning that they had to coordinate their efforts closely.

His letter of February 18, 1952 provides a case in point.

I'm sharing some important messages with you here, something that once again is time-sensitive…

I'm really sorry that we still have to get past some additional formalities, but it's not that bad, and you'll be able to get this done without any difficulties whatsoever.

Well, today I wanted to hand in our papers, and at that time I found out that they're not yet complete according to the newest regulations.

He then listed specific steps for her to follow as she navigated the thickets of bureaucracy.

We still need the formal support of the U.S. chaplain…This means that we have to have interviews…one together, and also separate interviews. I went to our chaplain right away, and he was really very friendly and immediately made a number of phone calls in connection with our situation—that is, because you're not here. Here's the solution, and I'm glad that people met me halfway like this. Please be so kind as to go the [in English] *Munich Military Post, Chaplains Branch* [in German] *and ask to speak with a Catholic chaplain. Don't be shy, because I know that you speak English very well and you're very businesslike. The chaplain is an actual man of the cloth in uniform, and he'll definitely be very friendly. This is approximately how I'd start to speak with him if I were you. After you ask to speak with a Catholic chaplain, don't say* [appellations in English] *"Sir" or "Mr." but rather address him as "Father." Something like this:* [in English, retaining Ernst's errors] *Father…I am Miss Liselotte Peschel and I am engaged to an American Soldier. My fiance, whos name is Ernst Roesch is presently stationed at the Berlin Military Post where he is a Corporal…In Berlin he was told by his Chaplain, Lt. Colonel Hlopko, that I should come to see you in regard to a pre-marriage interview. Would you please be so kind and speak to me and forward a report of this interview to my fiance in Berlin or to Father Hlopko, Berlin Military Post.* [in German] *And so on….*

You'll definitely be asked a lot of questions about who you are, your past, and your serious intentions with me. Be honest about everything, what you know about me and how we actually got to know each other—about our earlier correspondence and our current situation, and that we've been engaged since November 3rd.

Don't hesitate to say that you know Father Rosenberg very well and that this man also knows all about you. That can only help to make a good impression.

At the same time get the following: your baptism certificate and also mine…

Between the typed lines Ernst wrote the comment: *(Ask for two copies to be prepared.)*

Father Hlopko told me that you should confirm on the baptism certificate that you haven't been married before, because he'll definitely need that. He believes that this will be possible without any problems, which is news to me, but pay attention, and if it doesn't work out, then just get the baptism certificate there and get the rest from the police or a similar source. My other official papers already verify that I haven't been married before. As for my own baptism certificate, here are some details: It was in Munich, St. Joseph Church, and I think it was in the year 1931.

You know, you have to meet the priest halfway, because he has a lot of clout here, and these are the forms that he wants to have...

And so you see that I've made fairly extensive preparations, and people are willing to be flexible with us and make things easier for us.

In case you can't speak with a chaplain in Munich, then there's no other choice than for you to come to Berlin on a weekend and to do that very soon; then we'd go to church on Sunday and ask the priest after mass—that is, I'd already tell him beforehand that we'd be coming. But I don't think that that'll be necessary, because you only need to find out where the Catholic church for Americans is in Munich and just go there...

Well, I wish you lots of luck and success, my darling, and since both of us care for each other so very much, it won't be hard for you to make your confession. You can take along our engagement photo from Christmas as well as the one from König Lake.

Nor, by a long shot, were these steps the final ones.

February 29, 1952

<u>*My dear Liselotte!*</u>

Please be so kind as to fill out the [in English] *"Affidavit"* [in German] *that I've enclosed once again. (Complete the form three times.) After doing that, go to the* [in English] *Legal Assistance Officer, Munich Military Post* [in German] *and ask him to sign it. You need to be present, because you'll have to swear that everything on the form is valid. Then be so kind as to send it to me right away. Everything else with the chaplain went well. Beyond that, fill out this criminal records form and let it be validated at the same place where you got the character reference. If that doesn't work, then just send it back to me unsigned...*

Please excuse this hasty scribbling. I'm standing on the street as I write this.

They were married in the *Stadtpfarrkirche Christkönig*, a small Catholic church in the Nymphenburg section of Munich, on

October 14, 1952. Two children, Hans and Monika Sollfrank, carried Liselotte's veil at the ceremony. Years later two framed pictures of the parish church graced their bedroom wall.

Another black-and-white photo in our home showed Ernst and Liselotte as they exited the church, grinning at the camera as they prepared to climb into a horse-drawn carriage.

Our mother often reflected that, compared to modern weddings that she later attended in the States, theirs was a relatively quick and simple affair with none of the fancy rehearsals and preparations that often seemed to be de rigueur in America.

Their wedding reception took place at the posh *Hotel Vier Jahreszeiten*; Liselotte's sister Käthe was apparently envious that Karl Peschel had spent more on this affair than he had when she'd married her husband Walter. That might well have been because Liselotte would soon be leaving the country, maybe for good, and Karl wanted not merely to celebrate their wedding day but also give them an appropriate send-off for their transatlantic voyage in a few months' time.

On their honeymoon they rode the train to scenic locations in Switzerland and Italy, including Lugano and Milan. Judging from the plethora of photographs they snapped and then took great care to organize and preserve, the Milan cathedral was especially fascinating for them.

As much as I can tell now, there'll be enough to live on...

After their honeymoon they once again lived apart from each other. Ernst continued his work with military intelligence in Berlin; Liselotte lived in Munich.

The financial deliberations in their correspondence now grew more detailed. Ernst's draft for their budget reflected his hopes to buy a car as well as the need to support Amalie. On October 30, 1952, he noted that *the time it takes to save for a car would be about two years, if the savings we already have aren't taken into account.*

He offered several options for their budget, one that included fifty dollars earmarked for Amalie each month.

The amount of money per month for rent is about seventy-five dollars. All of the other expenditures remain as they are. Assuming that we use what we've saved so far to make a five-hundred-dollar down payment for a ten-thousand-dollar house, which we pay off, like rent, at the rate of seventy-five dollars per month, then this is what we've got:

$10,000.00
-500.00
9,500.00

This remaining amount, when it's split up into amounts of seventy-five dollars, means 127 months, or about ten years, and after that we'd both have our own house...However, our annual savings for these ten years can only amount to a mere six hundred dollars, which means that it'd take three more years to get a car while paying for the house. At the same time we can't forget that as soon as we buy a car, the monthly expenditures will go up by about fifty dollars, meaning that our annual savings will be pretty much zero.

Comments:

Assuming that we've already gotten a car and live in a rented apartment that costs us fifty dollars per month, then we'd need 275 dollars each month for sure.

In the same letter Ernst also shared auspicious news about his employment at Super Mold, something that made their goal of home ownership far more realistic.

Today I got more news from Mom and also a letter from Eddie, in which he sends both of us his sincere congratulations. In another one of Eddie's letters, which I received on Monday, he let me know, among other things, that my firm is really looking forward to my return, because certain construction problems have cropped up and they want to give me these problems to work on—and only me, apparently. From what I could tell from Eddie's words, it had to do with a move on the part of management against my boss, because it apparently became clear that there haven't been any new developments since I left, and that seems to make the chief engineer look bad. But, as I said, I have to wait and see what my situation will actually be...Beyond that, in the meantime I've worked out a way to set up a budget...When I have the chance, I'll let you know about this. As much as I can tell now, there'll be enough to live on and at the same time there'll be enough to save something. Of course, this suggestion is subject to the improvements that you might have, and also the pay raises that I'll hopefully get as time goes on.

Ernst then asked Liselotte to engage in what amounted to some low-key industrial espionage. Apparently it wasn't the first time that he'd approached her about doing something like this.

I don't know what you were able to do with regard to finding out about those machines. In connection with this I have another request. In Munich—Schwabing, I'm not sure where, exactly—there's a firm called ZÄNGL. They produce vulcanizing machines. Maybe you can get brochures with pictures and technical specifications from them. Especially interesting for me are the so-called "record heaters." Please, when you're asking about this, don't mention the name "Roesch," because they've already seen that name in overseas correspondence asking about the same things.

Of course, I'm only asking you to do this if it can be done without much difficulty.

He was also keen to remind her that *there are only twenty-six days until we actually leave.*

I'd really be very happy if I could travel together with you.

A few days later, on November 5, 1952, Liselotte summed up where her preparations stood.

That means that today was the crucial day when I got the travel visa for the States. I sent the completed forms to you right away, on Wednesday at 11:30. This morning I had to wait again for about two hours, but everything's on track as far as that's concerned. I hope that these forms reach you soon and in good condition so that the powers that be can take up my case...Above all, when we have the order—or the ship's order, I think that's the right way to say it—in our hands, I hope that we also find out something about packing...I hope that this also still keeps working out for us, because so far, again and again, we've had luck in spite of dealings with bureaucracies and other problems that have come up.

Finances were still playing a central role in her thoughts.

I'd really be very happy if I could travel with you. It'd be reassuring in some ways. That way we could also save some money, and that's also essential. You know, I don't want to be tightfisted when we're together in the

future, and I don't want to count every penny and maybe scrimp and save—
no, that wouldn't be nice, and that wouldn't be a life at all. It also, above all,
wouldn't make for a nice home for you, but setting up a budget and keeping
track of expenses is something that I'd do here and over there as well. It really
helps when you see how money is being spent…

Now, my dear Ernst, I'll repeat the numbers once again just in case you
weren't able to read something clearly…

Visa Number 87/6 issued on November 5, 1952
Passport Number A 108337/52, issued on October 28, 1952, valid until
October 28, 1957

I intentionally asked for the passport to be issued this way because
otherwise I'd have to go to a German consulate next March to ask for an
extension; my old one would have expired around this time. But this way
I hope that I'll be able to get American citizenship within this time frame.

When Ernst got the lowdown about their passage across the
Atlantic, he apprised Liselotte without delay.

November 11, 1952

Well, I'll let you know right away what I took care of yesterday and how
our plan looks now. Of course, what follows depends on the confirmation,
which I might get as soon as tomorrow.

Departure: December 8th 1952, from Bremerhaven
Arrival: December 17th 1952; New York, N.Y.
Ship: U.S. transport ship "General Darby"
Length of time in Bremen: Unknown as of this point
Your Accommodation in Bremen: [in English] American Dependent Hotel
Your Accommodation Immediately Following Our Arrival Over There: Fort
Hamilton, N.Y.
My Location During This Time: Camp Kilmer, N.J. for about twenty-four
hours

Just as they'd lived for quite a while in separate parts of the world—and then in different German cities—they'd now be assigned to different sections of the ship.

I can also tell you these details: We'll most likely be going across the Atlantic on the same ship, but we won't be together, of course, because you'll get a much better cabin along with other women.

But I'm especially looking forward to the moment when I can introduce you to my mother...

Upon their arrival in the States they'd also have to tolerate being separated for a time.

Immediately after our arrival you'll travel along with all of the other women to Fort Hamilton, a barracks, while I'll go with the troops to another barracks. There I'll receive my travel papers, etc. to go to Fort Ord, California, along with the six days of vacation that are still coming to me, on top of the five days of travel time. To say this another way, eleven days after leaving Camp Kilmer I'll have to report in at Fort Ord, and I'll stay there until I'm discharged on January 8, 1953. That means that I'll have eleven days to pick you up from Fort Hamilton and bring you to Lodi. As I said, we'll get to our new home in time for Christmas. We'll be able to spend this holiday together, and I'll be able to be with you for these initial days at least, and then I'll have to leave you for a week until I can finally be with you permanently.

We could also have traveled on November 30th, but I preferred December 8th because that way I'll be here for one more payday, and that also means that we won't be separated as long over there...

It's not yet clear that I'll be allowed to pick you up in Munich after Bremerhaven. It's possible that I'll then have to pay for the travel expenses myself, but that shouldn't cost anything for you...I also have to get the orders before the end of next week so that I can still go to Munich before then and oversee the packing and shipping of the [in English, retaining his spelling] *Houshold-good.*

He especially relished the prospect of getting to California and introducing Liselotte to Lodi—and to Amalie.

We'll get to Sacramento in the middle of the day, and I'm not quite sure myself how things will go on from there. Maybe we'll wait for a connecting train, or we'll continue our journey in a bus, or we'll make a phone call and let Eddie or Rivinius pick us up in their car, because it's only an hour's drive from Sacramento to Lodi. I'm glad that we're arriving during the winter, because right now the climate over there is similar to the climate here, maybe a little milder, and if it doesn't give you the impression of "sunny California" off the bat, well, then it gives you the chance to get acclimatized slowly. That'll also be a good thing for me, because I've also just spent one-and-a-half years in a more rugged climate again and my blood also needs to become thinner. But I'm especially looking forward to the moment when I can introduce you to my mother—when I can say, "Mama, this is my wife!" She'll certainly be very happy—yes, very glad that we're there at last—and when you see that you're very welcome there you'll certainly feel at ease right away. I'm only a little scared because Mama always cooks so much there and I probably won't be in the mood to eat a lot. I'll be so excited and happy that I've finally brought you to your new home.

Traveling right before the holiday season was something else that Ernst bore in mind.

Now something occurs to me that I have to talk with you about. It'll be Christmas when we get there, and I think that we can make an exception to the rule and avoid all of the gift giving. Something that we can't avoid is sending lots of Christmas cards. I think it'd certainly be best if you could make sure to keep the address list for our engagement announcements and take it along. Then, when we're in New York, we can buy a stack of Christmas cards, and we'll keep ourselves busy on the train by writing them, and signing them [in English] *"Mr. and Mrs. Ernst Roesch."* [in German] *I hope that you've still got the list, but if you don't, then it's not that bad, and I'll just have to strain my brain once more, for a change.*

Liselotte began her next letter with down-to-earth matters.

November 13, 1952

My dear Ernst, good evening!

I hope that you've already been able to finish up your duties for today, and that you're now at home inside your four walls. Maybe you're writing to me at this very moment. If not, then I'll visit you a bit through my thoughts—which through these words are especially close to you—and say a very nice hello to you. Do you also have lots of snow? Here there's one snow flurry after the other. Because of that it's also quite nippy; it usually freezes in the evening. If you do come, please dress in really warm clothes. Think about all of the advice that I've given you. It's really necessary; otherwise you'll freeze. I'm already wearing my rabbit fur coat; that one's really very warm. I'm still not sure if I want to take it along on the trip. What do you think? Otherwise my mother will get it; she can make good use of it here. I can't wear it over there, because it's not that cold there, and I don't know if I could use it if I go skiing or drive to the mountains.

It's too bad that she cried the way she did...

Saying goodbye to friends and acquaintances in Munich proved to be more difficult than she'd anticipated.

Today I visited my parents. Yesterday I said goodbye to Mrs. Ganter; she wanted to meet with me one more time. It was very nice yesterday evening. She was very sad that I was going away. She told me that she'd spoken with you in front of the church. Also, she asked me to let you know that you should take good care of me, etc. You can imagine that she really likes me a lot, even though she was my boss and we didn't see each other outside of work. And—yes, she also told me that I shouldn't forget to watch out for myself and take care of myself…Beyond that, she was hoping to get news from me and to get photographs, which I'll send her while I'm still here. She liked all of the pictures a lot. She also said that everything looked so good in the church.

It's too bad that she cried the way she did, because when we said goodbye to each other it also really got to me. She's really sincerely fond of me—it's not a role that she's playing, I know that much.

When she took her leave of co-workers at her firm, she met with some unexpected and coarse comments.

On Tuesday I was in my previous firm, and among other things I showed the photos, and I also had to thank them. Everyone was very cordial, but also very curious, and no less envious, but that didn't affect me. I didn't even respond to some of the rude questions—you can imagine the sort of questions that they were—because I think that's so nasty and mean. Besides that, I easily blush, but there are just people who enjoy using such rude expressions. I have to say that I felt very distant from everything there, and I could barely believe that I'd actually left that firm on September 9, 1952. Since then so many new things—so many other things—have come into my life that I've become fully immersed in them and haven't thought about the Holz Berufsgenossenschaft [her former workplace] *any longer.*

Ernst sought to comfort her about the unpleasant scene at her firm.

November 17, 1952

As I see from your words, you're very busy visiting people and saying goodbye to them. I know how stressful that is. It's awful enough that your former female colleagues asked such intrusive questions. But I've already heard once that things like that often happen, that people give a young woman the third degree that way—yes, that they want to find out about the most personal things from her.

In her November 13th letter she also assured him that she'd take her role and responsibility as his wife seriously.

I don't know how it'll be when I'm over in the States later on. But I think that when I can actually be in our home and I try to make everything nice and comfortable for the two of us there, then I'll soon feel fulfilled. More than anything else I want you to be completely satisfied and happy with your wife, that you also feel content, and above all, that you're always glad when you come home in the evening, because that's the only way that things can really be good for me.

In the midst of all of their preparations to leave Germany a mini-crisis transpired—one involving Marko, Therese Reiner's dog.

Yesterday I couldn't get to sleep that fast because Marko had run away at 5:30 in the morning and he still wasn't back at eleven at night. And so Gisela and I went looking for him and then we found him, totally freezing. Right now he's having problems in his love life. He's suffering terribly, and he must have had very cold feet when he was with his beloved because he actually had spheres of ice on his feet, the poor guy! Overjoyed and very hungry and thirsty—and also contrite and frozen through and through—he went back home. I really felt so sorry for him, and then as a reward he got a dog biscuit from me—but only because we were so happy that he's back with us, is what both of us said, laughing. I really only got to sleep at midnight.

Ernst's letter of November 14, 1952 shared details of their passage to the United States and reflected vastly improved typing abilities.

My dear Liselotte - and dear wife!

I just got a phone call letting me know that our place on the ship has been changed. We'll have to be in Bremerhaven by November 30th.

And so -   My arrival in Munich: the 27th or 28th of November
Our departure from Munich: November 29th, 1952
Ship's departure: December 2, 1952

Enclosed in the envelope are forty German marks.

For today I'm sending you many affectionate greetings,
I'm in a hurry, but—with a very dear kiss—always
[handwritten] *your Ernst* [typed] *who loves you.*

I'm now really waiting on you to tell me the definite news...

During these intricate travel preparations Liselotte suspected that she was pregnant. Ernst wanted to make very sure that her concerns about money wouldn't stop her from seeking out the medical care that she needed.

November 14, 1952

My dear Liselotte and my dear wife!

Today I got your dear words from the eleventh of November. I want to thank you a lot for them. Your letter's content is, once again, especially lovely and heartfelt, and I'll deal with all of the things that you brought up, but I'll begin with the most important thing...

Unfortunately, it's no longer possible for me to get the necessary German marks this evening. But tomorrow I'll try to get them and then send them to you right away. But I ask that you definitely go to the doctor today—that is, to this particular woman doctor. I'm very sorry that you've become stressed because of a situation that still isn't clear for either of us, and I especially can't let you hesitate to go to the doctor because of financial concerns, etc. So please do this without further delay, because for you it's definitely very important and, yes, it's also important for me. And so now I've made things clear, and now I can begin to respond to this in a somewhat more mellow tone. So I'm asking you not to get upset at all, even if I'm not in a position to speak about this matter, but I can at least sympathize...and so you can also trust me...I'm only writing this—not so that the message is, that's a woman's situation, period—but because in spite of that I'm actually as involved in this as you are. Since I read about this news, I've already lit up a third cigarette...I'm now really waiting on you to tell me the definite news, and I hope that you'll keep me up to date about what's happening. I'd certainly be very happy if it were really true, but I ask you to understand that my primary concern, without a doubt, is my dear wife's health and happiness. And so I urge you to go to the doctor because, first, it's certainly a very good idea for you to find out for sure about your condition, and, beyond that, in case it really is a delay, for you to find out more about your situation...Besides, as a newlywed woman you can definitely learn all sorts of things when you're there, things that would benefit both of us a lot, especially because we're really experiencing and feeling something completely new when it comes to such things. It's certainly wonderful to experience all of this in such a mysterious way—yes, I wouldn't have it any other way. But that's just the way it is, that precisely in this new phase of life things happen like what's happening now with you. They're so mysterious that they lead to nervous tension—something that a skillful physician's counsel might be able to stop. And so I'm really insisting that you go to the doctor, and don't worry about paying for the appointment because when all is said and done that's my concern.

It's very possible that the deck will offer the only chance for us to see each other...

Money was tight in the final days leading up to their departure in early December.

November 15, 1952

My dear Liselotte!

To begin with, here's the newest information about the future that we'll soon have together. Well, I've just applied for a passport, and it now looks as if I'll meet you early on Thursday, November 20th. Then I'll travel back to Berlin early on Saturday. I hope that you have everything ready to be packed, because we want to take care of that in these two days.

As I've already shared with you very briefly, our travel date's been changed, and I'll get to Munich at 6:30 in the evening on November 27th to pick you up. Then we'll travel to Bremerhaven together on November 29th, because we need to be there on the 30th. The way things look now, the ship will leave on December 2nd. That means that the dates have been moved up. I was told that, because I want to pick you up, I'll have to pay for my trip to Munich and then to Bremerhaven myself, but there's nothing to be done about that. It's just good that we at least got permission to do this. On the other hand, there's a chance that your trip from Munich to Bremerhaven won't cost anything. I haven't taken a closer look at the train schedule yet, but I think that the eleven o'clock military train (we can't go on any others, because then you'd also have to pay for sure) definitely has a connection in Frankfurt—that is, we can go from there to Bremerhaven in a sleeping car. That means that you'll get your wish—that you won't have to say "Goodbye" on this train, but that this time you'll be able to ride with me, even though there'll still be the general ambiance of leave-taking.

I've just telegraphed about money today. Since our travel date has been moved up, I don't have a payday to look forward to here anymore, and I'd been counting on that in my plans. Hopefully this money will arrive here soon, because I'm waiting for it frantically. As far as the voyage itself is concerned, I don't really know myself how much carry-on luggage you can have, but anyway it's limited by the amount that you can carry, and so, at most, it's two suitcases. In my case I can only have one suitcase—that means one piece of luggage, and so I'll probably take along Miss Reiner's suitcase. We'll probably be separated on the ship, though I'll still see if we can get a cabin for the two of us—but that can only be arranged in Bremerhaven.

As I've said, everything has gone very well so far, and so let's continue to trust our good luck. I'll certainly do what I can to make everything as comfortable for you as possible, because even that way it'll be a stressful trip—it's such a long one. I advise you to take along a headscarf for the ship for sure, because it's always cold on deck and this is the only practical thing you can do about that. It's very possible that the deck will offer the only chance for us to see each other for a few hours each day, because I'll actually still be on duty, and I'll have to work somewhere. Besides that, I'll be located far down below in the ship, etc. You, on the other hand, will be traveling in a better class. You'll be together with maybe two other women in a cabin, and you'll eat in a better dining hall—you know, along with the other women and the officers. It's a really odd arrangement, and many American women have already gotten upset about it. In this connection I've heard about cases of self-help.

Ernst had a scheme in mind to see more of Liselotte when they were en route to America, and it wasn't without some risk.

The three women who were sharing one cabin would arrange things so that two of them would always take a walk on the deck for an hour in the evening and watch out for the military police. Meanwhile the husband of the third woman would try to get into his wife's quarters without being caught so that he could at least speak with her for a little while—because things aren't very private up on deck. I'm not sure if that should be seen as romantic or adventurous, and, what's more, the husband risks being caught and getting punished. But then I've also heard that if extra cabins are available, married men are allowed to live there with their wives, and so we still can hope for that.

Ernst sorely missed Liselotte's presence—sometimes for very pragmatic and mundane reasons.

My dear wife: everywhere your husband looks, he notices how much he misses his wife. The buttons of my shirt are torn off; some clothing articles need to be mended. Everywhere there are things missing. Please—may I bring you my drill jacket on Thursday so that you can sew the stripes on while I'm gone again? Also, the nylon shirt hasn't been washed yet. Please do that for me as well. I've already decided to take along the good blue suit in my carry-on luggage. Then I'll definitely have it along at Christmas—and, in addition, the nylon shirt that you'll certainly take care of for me. So please, please—be so kind as to take care of these things...

Now, unfortunately, I have to wrap up this letter, because I'm being interrupted again, and so I'll say "Good Night" right away for today, because I won't get back to do more writing later on. And so, once again, a really good kiss, a dear heartfelt embrace—and sleep well, my darling.

Always with love,
Your fortunate husband,
Your Ernst.

Liselotte wrote most of her next letter a few hours before her doctor's appointment.

November 16th and 17th, 1952

Good morning, my beloved Ernst!
I wanted to start writing this to you half an hour ago, but then I checked the mailbox to see if the morning mail had already gotten here. Then the doorbell rang, and your registered letter arrived. Thanks so much for everything. Today I was able to pay the doctor from what I had left over, because I've made a budget and really just spent what was absolutely necessary. But I hope that you don't have problems because you gave me this money. Anyway, thanks so much. I'll be able to go to the doctor today at two in the afternoon. Yesterday I met her by accident. I'll be very happy when I finally know what I should do—and above all what the cause of this is. I haven't been feeling very well for ten to twelve days now, but that's not the only reason for this because everything else—you know what I mean, saying goodbye—is also

very much inside me, and when I'm saying goodbye to someone I definitely always think too much about it later on. Most of all in the evening, before I fall asleep, I just can't simply lie quietly, and so the unconscious is also hard at work during the night, so that the sleep I get is a little restless. Sometimes I wake up in the morning with a headache, but I hope and also know that this will settle down after a while over there. The time that's coming now will certainly be a test for me, because I'll have to deal with many things inside myself—even as I'm also very thankful when you try to help me with this. Please, please, my dear Ernst, don't be irritated about these words. I'm sure that you can understand them a little. I don't mean them with respect to our life together later on, because I firmly believe that we'll understand each other well and above all I trust, really fully trust, my husband, who has really been always so understanding and sympathetic up to now. But you already know what's now coming ever closer. That affects me a lot emotionally, even though on the outside I'm unchanged—aside from food, but the women I live with already know about that. I'm definitely very lucky that it's possible for us to travel together...

My dear Ernst, half an hour ago I got your news that we'll already leave from here—or, to be more exact, from Bremerhaven—on December 2, 1952. You'll need to be here on November 28th at the latest, and we'll leave here on November 29th, 1952. Please excuse me if I'm writing this way, but right now I'm somehow not feeling well; I'm feeling a little dizzy. But still, I ask you, don't be upset with me, because you know that it can be this way, and you also know that I've figured out the weeks and Sundays and everything already very precisely. Now I'll have to start getting used to the fact that we'll have to leave here in a week from this coming Saturday...

After I go to the doctor today, I'll put a note into this envelope right away so that you'll know what's happening. I'll have to wait until the afternoon to send off the letter, but in any case it'll probably start its journey to you tomorrow. I hope that I'll be able to give you good news. It's clear that this uncertain condition, which is psychologically very unsettling for me, can be cleared up this afternoon, and hopefully that'll have a big effect on everything else. It's too bad that I have this now, but hopefully I'll soon find out what the cause is.

As it turned out, Liselotte was in fact pregnant with Ursula, my older sister.

In connection with this I want to thank you above all so much for your words of understanding. They really helped me a lot. I'll definitely never think that it's just something for women, because you, my husband, are certainly involved in this.

She was already bracing herself for the culture shock that was bound to happen when she arrived in California.

I'll just need some time until I've adjusted to everything mentally.

Most of all, I hope, when we've gotten there and maybe even have our own apartment, that I'll handle my duties the way I did at work—that I'll take care of them to my complete satisfaction and also yours. You know, I'm the sort of person who's quickly dissatisfied with herself if I can't get something done or accomplish something the way that I imagined it should be. This kind of ambition and effort is definitely something positive when you're on the job, and I also want to put it to use in my new environment...

An uncomfortable encounter at the post office reminded Liselotte of the hostility that some other Germans felt about her relationship with an American soldier.

When I went to send off the letter at the post office on Ludwig Street...the clerk was so rude: he told me that I had to pay for international postage. I just told him that I'd take my letter back and bring it to another post office. But he went to his boss right away, and then three of them talked about this problem. Unfortunately the people waiting in line behind me had to wait longer. But one very friendly older man stood up for me and grumbled about the typical German bureaucracy. In the end it turned out that I was right, even though the clerk didn't admit it, but he said instead that he was just making an exception and that I'd have to use international stamps on all of my letters. I was pretty upset—not on the outside, on the outside I was completely calm—but inside I was pretty furious when I went to the streetcar. Everything can happen to you. The worst was that he always said, so politely, "Miss" to me...I told him very clearly that I was your wife. I just hope that the letter will soon get to you; then everything will be all right.

Ernst's temper flared when he read about the incident.

So, you have to admit that it now really seems to be going smoothly; at least I'm satisfied. I'm glad, because that helps a person...to say goodbye to such impolite people as the postal clerk on Ludwig Street. If something like that happened again and I was there, I'm not sure if I wouldn't become openly angry.

In her November 16th and 17th letter Liselotte also wrote candidly about the feelings going through her mind.

My dear Ernst, I have to confess to you honestly, that when I got the visa...I left the building with mixed feelings. I was very happy—yes, I actually breathed a sigh of relief because I had finally gotten this time of waiting behind me. On the other hand, I realized the enormous change that will soon come upon me. But I hope and continue to trust my lucky star, because up to now I've already had luck in my life, and hopefully that won't leave me when I'm living far away, where I'll be especially dependent on luck.

I hope that you understand these words about luck correctly, but I won't be able to fully take advantage of everything that you're offering me—and enjoy it—unless I feel completely at home, I'm healthy, and I feel really happy and content about my new set of tasks and my new life. I think you'll agree with me about this. There are many things, especially right at the start, that I'll have to deal with on my own, even when I talk about them with you and you notice when I'm sad or when I'm happy. You know, dear Ernst, yesterday I heard a lot again about what some people who are going to America imagine about life over there. They're full of passionate enthusiasm. As far as I'm concerned, they're overdoing it...Being the sort of person that I am, I'm going over there with a very sensible attitude, very reflectively, and not expecting anything in particular. I'd rather let myself be surprised at what I find.

The sheer number of letters that they exchanged during these weeks is striking.

November 17, 1952

...My passport's been approved in the meantime. Just as before, I'm planning to be with you on Thursday morning. If I don't get there then, then wait for me on Thursday evening, because right now, once again, it's tough

to find a way to travel to you. *Tomorrow I'll also be waiting for our travel papers for Bremerhaven and the U.S.A., and then I'll take them with me to Munich. And so it's the same as it's been so far:* Departure from Munich: November 28, 1952.

And now I want to thank you a lot for your dear letter of the fourteenth of the month. In that letter you once again presented everything in a very affectionate way, and your words did me a lot of good...I don't think that I'm in the right state of mind today to write a nice and fitting response for its especially precious content...

I've just bought Christmas cards, and I'll bring them along for you. Maybe we can write all of them before we leave. Of course, we'll only do that—writing out all of these addresses—if it's possible for you time-wise. But, you know, then we'd send them off from here and we'd have gotten this task behind us...

Of course I can understand that your mother's asking about it, because of course when all is said and done she's concerned about her daughter's health and happiness, and she wants to find out about this. Beyond that, as a woman she knows that this sort of contentment can do a lot for a marriage, and that it can definitely influence a woman's state of mind. I don't think that you went into detail about things, but I hope that you told your mom some things so that she could get the impression that her son-in-law is the right man for her daughter.

As some snapshots verify, Ernst and Liselotte were indeed able to spend some quality time together during the passage to America.

Whether Ernst ever actually ignored his duties on board and eluded the MPs to spend time with Liselotte, as he suggested to her in one of his letters, is unclear.

After they arrived in New York City, they only spent a few days there before traversing the continent by train. Soon after getting to Lodi they moved into an apartment on North Crescent Avenue.

My older sister Ursula was born on July 20, 1953. A Christmas photo from that year shows my parents with Ursula. On the left, standing guard in front of the curtains, is one of Karl Peschel's lamps. Exactly how they'd managed to transport it from Germany to their new apartment in Lodi remains, like many other things, something of a mystery, but it was a fixture in our home for decades, a beacon and a sturdy friend, continuing to function reliably until well into the new millennium.

Karl Peschel passed away soon afterwards, but for several years Liselotte maintained close contact with her mother through letters. In one of them she apparently shared her thoughts about Ursula, and then added that she only wanted to have one child and no more. In her response on December 12, 1953, Liselotte's mother made no bones about her views.

I don't fully understand why you're giving away your maternity dresses. You're still young, and you still don't know if you'll be able to use them yourself—but you already seem to be convinced about that!

Her mother's nudging, here and elsewhere, was probably one factor that led her to reconsider her thoughts. And so Ursula wound up with three siblings, and the tapestry of my own early family memories became possible.

CHAPTER NINE

Farewells

Du hast mich lieb!

*I*n the early Seventies, without warning, Therese Reiner phoned Liselotte from Germany. She wanted very much to see Liselotte once again and invited her to come over to visit her in Munich; she'd also help to defray the costs of the trip.

Even though our father had reservations about it, our mother took her up on her offer. Soon she was spending a few weeks in Germany visiting with Frau Reiner along with other close friends—including Hermann John, someone she'd also kept in touch with over the years.

Her choice to meet with Herr John again precipitated a dark period on our parents' marriage, something that weighed on our family for months. Arguments flared between them in the evenings and on the weekends. Our father would sometimes take out the accordion files that held their old correspondence and then read and reread the old letters that he and our mother had sent to each other, basking nostalgically in the spirit and warmth of those earlier times.

That habit, though, and the comments he made about what she'd written and promised him, only led to fresh rounds of recriminations. I suspect that this is when our mother began taking a pair of scissors to much of the correspondence and editing it so thoroughly. She didn't want him, as she saw it, to keep weaponizing her words, hurling accusations at her about what she'd written back then and how she'd changed since then.

During that time Dad and I had maintained our practice of taken a postprandial walk around Willow Glen on most evenings. One autumn evening, when he reminded me that my birthday was coming up soon and asked me what I wanted for my special day, I told him that I just wanted him to go to a marriage counselor with my mother. My wish blindsided him, and when he hedged and then refused our talk quickly darkened. At one point, while I was in the middle of a sentence, he just turned on his heel and began heading back to our house on his own. A few minutes later, when I met him in the vestibule of the house, I tried to press my point, but he refused to hear me out.

Soon, though, they did seek out the support of a counselor, and they started seeing her regularly. My mother kept me apprised from time to time about those sessions; I imagine that she kept my siblings in the picture to some extent as well. During one session our father wanted to talk about sex, something that she clearly found difficult to talk about openly with a third party at first. Later on, she let me know that the therapist had started meeting one-on-one with Dad, "preparing him"—as the therapist phrased it—"to get divorced." That proved to be a traumatic struggle for him, given his strict Catholic upbringing and, on top of that, the anguish he'd felt when his own parents had separated.

How did my parents find their way back to one another? Only a few letters and postcards seem to have come from Hermann John after this time, so it could be that their relationship started to heal as our mother elected to distance herself from the close and dear friend of her youth. Once, when our family was on vacation at Lake Tahoe, I remember seeing them strolling along the sidewalk hand in hand—something unusual because they typically didn't display affection that openly. It seemed very much to be a strategy that our mother used to mollify him. We'd overheard him saying that he wanted to hold hands with her in public, the way other couples did, and she acquiesced to his wishes and kept on doing this from time to time.

Among the operatic gems that both of them cherished was *The Merry Widow*; in fact, their CD collection of operas boasted not one, but two complete recordings of Franz Lehar's comic masterpiece. One key moment in the libretto features a duet in which the two main characters, Danilo and Hanna, celebrate their attraction to each other, a moment that leads to their decision to marry. At the close of their duet they both sing:

> *Every time our hands touched*
> *Showed me clearly*
> *That it's true, it's so true—*
> *You love me!*

The melodies and sentiments of Lehar's work as well as those of other operas—not to mention their shared love of nature—certainly played a role in helping them to mend their troubled relationship. Our father's faltering health also changed the way they acted toward each other; he came to rely on her in ways that he hadn't needed to earlier.

The wealth that you actually have in your life can't be measured in money.

In the mid-Eighties, maybe because his initial heart attack in 1984 reminded him of his mortality, our father bought four copies of George Samuel Clason's *The Richest Man in Babylon*, one for each of us children, and presented them to us in a somber, ceremonial way. On a blank page toward the front of each paperback he'd composed an individual letter, hoping that he could influence us to take our financial decisions seriously. The one he wrote to me, a composite of English and German, and made up almost exclusively of precisely printed letters, read like this:

TO MY SON, STEVEN:
[in German] *By way of an introduction I want to say:*

1. *Money isn't the common denominator of wealth.*
2. *The wealth that you actually have in your life can't be measured in money.*
3. *Earning money doesn't make you happy; it's a necessity in our civilization.*

[in English] *May the stories in this book stimulate cautious and effective management of your monetary earnings, large or small.*
With the very best wishes, always,
Your Dad
Lodi, Calif., December 1986

As his health declined, our father began showing some disturbing signs of frailty now and then. On one especially difficult morning he carried his bowl of breakfast oatmeal from the kitchen over to the dining room, and he had to go slowly, holding onto the bowl gingerly to make it that far. It was a major ordeal just to get to his chair.

On the other hand, he didn't go gently into the dark night. Photos carefully arranged and captioned in a black three-ring binder document some of the trips he took in the last few years of his life. Our parents drove to Yosemite on July 9, 1986, and they hiked to Lembert Dome—9,450 feet, as he recorded proudly in one of his captions. In October 1986 they went to Carmel and Monterey for a few days and spent some memorable hours strolling along the rugged California coastline.

In late November both of them went up to Yosemite again, and on the 22nd they managed to complete the hike from Yosemite Valley up to Glacier Point. February 1987 found them spending a few days' time at Badger Pass. Our father apparently didn't ski on that outing, but the pictures show his contentment and his appreciation of the natural beauty around them. The last time they got up to Yosemite, as far as I can tell, was in March 1987.

Dad also managed to complete the Bay to Breakers marathon on May 17, 1987. One of the final photographs in the binder shows him crossing the finish line, clad in jogging pants and a white sweatshirt, a blue cap adorning his head—probably one that our mom had knitted for him—and a card with the number 19108 on his chest.

During June and July that year our parents flew back to Germany, visiting key tourist sites as well as sites of personal importance, such as Therese Reiner's gravesite and the church where they were married.

In October 1987 they celebrated their anniversary at Carmel. In November 1988 they went on a day hike at Jeffrey Pine. Around this time they also took an extended trip to the Canadian Rockies and toured Banff and Lake Louise, among other locations. Dad was clearly eager to chalk up more hiking accomplishments to add to the ones he'd garnered during his early years in California in the late Forties.

About a week before he was struck with a third and fatal heart attack, I drove up to Lodi to visit both them as well as Ursula. Barbara had moved out to an apartment in Stockton, which meant that her bedroom was now vacant—opening up the possibility for Dad to set up his own office there. That Saturday afternoon I helped him get the place ready, moving some of Barbara's things out into the garage and then helping him put up some shelves for his collection of technical reference books. We must have made quite a racket, at least now and then, because my mother and Ursula both let us know, again and again, how noisy we were. They insisted that we quiet down—after all, it was a weekend afternoon—but Dad and I were so preoccupied with our task that we pretty much ignored them. Somehow we'd discovered a rhythm to our work that suited both of us and held us in its sway. We had a job to do, we were going to complete it, and if that meant getting loud, well, the neighbors and anyone else close by would just have to deal with it. When I left that evening, the new shelves were already in place on three of the four walls, and Dad had already begun arranging his books on them.

He was one of a few hundred former Super Mold employees who attended a company reunion at the Jackson Hall in Lodi on June 16, 1990. The *Lodi News-Sentinel* article covering the event noted that "at one time Super Mold Corporation was one of the largest manufacturers of tire recapping and repairing equipment in the world." That evening he had a grand old time meeting with friends and colleagues, and the chance to see them again and relive their glory days meant a lot to him.

He passed away two days later, on June 18th.

Our father now lies buried in the Riverside National Cemetery in southern California. His grave marker identifies him properly as a corporal in the U.S. Army, but then erroneously includes Korea as the country where he served. Since his death in 1990 I've driven down to Riverside several times. Once, before getting onto the freeway, I clipped a number of roses from the bushes in my backyard and laid them into an ice chest to keep them in good shape. When I arrived at the cemetery about five hours later, I set them around the perimeter of his grave marker.

The last time I drove there, on August 25, 2017, I wasn't alone; Tom came along with me. My niece Mattie had begun a doctoral program in physical therapy at USC, and I'd driven down to Los Angeles to join him and his wife Rebecca at the white-coat ceremony for the new DPT cohort. The next day he and I headed out toward Riverside—with me behind the wheel of my VW Golf and Tom acting as co-pilot and navigator, using Google on his phone to guide me. It was a brisk, sunny morning, and only a few other visitors were at the cemetery besides us. We could stand at his grave and honor his memory in shared silence.

"I'll do it for you. I'd be happy to do it for you."

Our mother always took care of her health—physical, intellectual, and spiritual. At first we all failed to notice—or just shrugged off—some occasional signs of her mental decline.

Sometimes in the fall of 2006, when I brought her to Dr. Kummerfeld, her eye doctor, we had to spend quite a long time in his waiting room, and I took to bringing along a sudoku booklet to while away the time. She began taking an interest in what I was up to, and then—as was typical for her—she wanted to learn how to solve a sudoku puzzle on her own. I'd show her some basic strategies, and she'd listen intently to everything I said. Try as she might, though, she never got the hang of it, even with a book of beginners' puzzles that she bought later on at a supermarket in Lodi. Never could she identify which numbers went where to complete a sudoku grid.

Around the same time the subject of Einstein came up. She told us that she'd known Einstein when she was a young girl. He'd lived in the neighborhood, she claimed, and apparently his family and hers had often mingled in the same social circles. Her description was so vivid that at first I bought it completely. Then it hit me that things couldn't have happened that way. Einstein was born in Ulm in 1879, long before my mother, who was born in Munich—not Ulm—in 1927. Yet she still clung to that conviction in our later conversations. "I knew Einstein," she told me point-blank on many occasions.

As our mother's Alzheimer's took root and got progressively worse, Ursula and I found ourselves calling her "Lisa," the way that the neighbors in Lodi were doing, rather than "Mom." It made sense to do this, in retrospect. She'd become a different person, and as such a different name was warranted to match her new, diminished identity. Our mother had passed over a threshold. Her words and behavior had changed substantially, and the way she now acted led us to change the way we acted toward her, even the way we spoke with her and about her.

Due to her Alzheimer's her English now began to fail her, and Ursula and I decided that moving Lisa to a facility wasn't a realistic option. Living in a place where she couldn't readily communicate with the staff or fellow patients would be hellish, whereas staying in her own home—which she still recognized and felt comfortable in—would be far more manageable. During those months of home care we often tuned in to Capital Public Radio, the classical music station in Sacramento, and we kept it running in the background for hours each day for her. Although our mother hadn't watched much television as a rule in earlier years, reruns of *I Love Lucy, Little House on the Prairie,* and *The Golden Girls* now became staples of her daily routine.

When I drove up from Fresno to help Ursula with her caretaking, I always spoke to Lisa in German and read her texts by some of the titans of German prose and poetry. She still had a fair grasp of her native tongue, especially when it came to listening when others spoke or read to her *auf Deutsch.* For a time I chose some sections of Hesse's *Wanderung* for her, then switched to passages from the Goethe collection *Die Kunst des Lebens.* One section dealt with a time in Italy when Goethe and his friends watched and admired a herd of wild horses until the setting sun made it impossible to discern them anymore. Another involved an unlikely meeting between Goethe and Klopstock, another renowned German poet, in which they discussed ice skating, and Klopstock claimed that skating made you feel like the god Hermes, with wings on your feet. Lisa clearly enjoyed hearing this sort of material, and as she listened her own ability to understand and express herself improved, at least for a while.

The same thing happened when I read Goethe's poem *"Der Erlkönig"*; she understood the supernatural danger facing the father and son as they raced on horseback through the murky forest. Somehow we then settled on working our way through an old German prose version of *The Odyssey,* and during the last several months of her life I always read an excerpt to her every time that I came up to Lodi. She'd been fascinated with ancient Greece and Rome all of her life, and even now she recognized and relished many of Odysseus' adventures, in particular the tales of the Cyclops and the Sirens. We even got to the moment when Odysseus, in disguise, returns to Ithaca. Although people in his homeland initially fail to recognize him, his loyal dog Argos immediately knows who he is.

Before we finished the saga of Odysseus' homecoming, though, her life ended. We never reached the section where he's reunited with his wife Penelope and his son Telemachus. When we left off, he'd reached Ithaca, but he hadn't fully made it home.

It was a dream—or at least the tail section of a dream—that came to me while I was working on the final part of this manuscript. I was back in Lodi, visiting my parents in the Midvale house. I was sitting with my father at the dining room table and drinking coffee with him; as always, he sat at the head of the table with his arms supported comfortably on the armrests of his chair. Then I noticed the clock above the upright piano behind him. It was already four in the afternoon—time for me to get going. I remember thinking that I wanted to hit the road by, at the very latest, four-thirty.

And then I found myself in the living room, bright to the point of dazzling because of the open curtains and the strong afternoon sunlight pouring in. My mother was busy at housework, vacuum cleaning around the sofa and the armchairs with vigorous, firm strokes. She worked quickly, brimming with energy. When she became aware of me, she stopped and shut off the machine. I let her know that I had to go soon, and then also told her, "You don't have to do this work. I'll do it for you. I'd be happy to do it for you." Our eyes met, but then somehow she seemed distracted. She never spoke in the dream—nor had my father had actually said anything during our time over coffee in the next room.

Sometimes The Past is like another continent—vast, murky, and eerily distant. It's a collection of question marks, so wrapped up in the fog of semi-memories that it has no real shape and it can't ever be mapped. And then you recognize that The Past is here, in your midst, at your elbow. It's been a house guest all along, and you've gotten so used to its presence that you don't even see it much at all. A lot of the time it's invisible to you in the rush and tumble of days, and still it lingers and murmurs, observes and listens.

On top of one of the bookcases in my living room is the American flag that draped our father's coffin, the one that an American army officer presented to my mother at his funeral in Riverside.

The urn containing our mother's ashes stands in another bookcase next to the dining room table. Actually, it's not a traditional urn, but just a piece of pottery decked out in blue-and-white Bavarian colors and replete with a lid. Ursula, Tom, and I had found it in the house and figured it would be something that our mother would have appreciated and approved of. We brought it to the Cherokee Memorial Funeral Home in a plain brown paper bag, showed it the people working there to see how they'd react to our request—and it passed muster.

After our mother's death Ursula kept living in the house in Lodi. Despite Tom's and my efforts and those of her neighbors, she grew increasingly isolated. The alcoholic dependency that she'd already developed now deepened; it was her secret way of coping with the trauma of losing our mother and confronting the ghosts and troubling memories that inhabited all of those rooms. She'd become very adept at hiding her drinking habit from the rest of us, and for a long time we had no idea just how much trouble she was in. About five months after Lisa passed Ursula collapsed in the house. Thanks to the quick action of a neighbor, Steve Ronsko, she was found and brought to the emergency room at Lodi Memorial Hospital; subsequently she spent several months at the Vienna Nursing & Rehabilitation Center, where she learned how to live her life free of the scourge of alcohol and even how to walk again, at least for a while. Sadly, she never fully escaped her addiction, in spite of phases in which she desperately tried to break away from it. Her life became a tragic cycle of staying sober, starting to drink again on the sly, being rushed to the emergency room, and then undergoing treatment for weeks or months. That pattern came to an end one Saturday night in April 2016 when her weakness finally got the better of her.

I phoned her early on that Sunday morning from Fresno. When she didn't pick up, I left a message on her answering machine. When I still got her voice mail a few hours later, I contacted the police and asked them to check up on her. They got back to me about an hour after that with the news that they'd found her lying on her bed. They assured me that hers had been a peaceful death. When I came to the house a few days later, a nearly empty bottle of Asbach Uralt brandy stood on her bedside table.

According to the terms of the trust that Ursula had set up, the house would be given to another party, not anyone in the family. Tom and I were contacted and allowed to work in the house for a few days to gather up family mementos like photo albums and remove them from the premises, after which time the locks would be changed.

We'd packed up scores of bankers boxes and brought them out to a storage unit along Cherokee Lane. Our plan was to meet in a few months—he'd fly out to California again with his wife to help us—and sort through the boxes to decide what to do with their contents.

We tried to call our sister Barbara many times and wound up leaving a lot of voice mails on her cell phone. For quite a while, though, she'd been keeping her distance from the rest of the family, and—whether she was unable or unwilling—she didn't get out to Lodi to help us go through the rooms in the house.

The classical music stream on Capital Public Radio provided the soundtrack for our efforts in those days, and Tom and I found ourselves playing a guessing game that we all used to play years ago on family road trips. Back then we'd tuned into a classical music station on the car radio and typically land in the middle of a symphony, a concerto, some chamber music, or a solo piece. The challenge was to name the composer and, if possible, the specific work being performed. After everyone in the car ventured their best guess, we waited for the piece to end, at which point the announcer's voice would let us know which of us had come up with the right answer.

Once, while we were packing the bankers boxes, Tom correctly identified a piano concerto as Brahms's First. Another time he was sure that Capradio was playing Beethoven's Coriolan Overture, but I countered that it was actually his Egmont Overture. That time I won the round.

It was about four in the afternoon when we wrapped up our work in the family house—as best we could, given the time restrictions that we faced. He had to head up to Sacramento to catch his flight back to South Carolina; I needed to get back to Fresno and prep for my Edison High classes on the following day. We toured the rooms one last time—the dark and somber entrance hall and shadowy living room, the hallway leading back to the bedrooms. Even though we'd combed through the place and packed and brought out scores of boxes, there was a lot that we hadn't been able to get to—clothes, books, some of our father's technical materials, many of the wall ornaments. The last step was to switch off the radio and end the dulcet flow of concert music. We took our leave in front of the garage; Tom got into his rental car and pulled away first. I headed out a few minutes later, and before long I was moving down Highway 99.

It was a bright, windy afternoon, and a bank of mammoth clouds spanned across the western sky.

ACKNOWLEDGEMENTS

$\mathscr{R}$endering my parents' correspondence and related materials in English would have been well-nigh impossible without the support and advice of Runy Runge and Professor David Engle. Dr. Engle was especially helpful in showing me how to decipher some of the antiquated handwriting that I came across. For several weeks I was stymied by a cryptic caption underneath a picture taken in Bad Reichenhall—apparently something that my mother had written in shorthand. Then Gisela Baumgärtner, my cousin Thomas' wife in Munich, interpreted it for me with ease, and that mystery was solved.

Early sections of this book have their roots in talks that I gave about my parents at Manchester GATE in Fresno, and I'm deeply grateful to all of the instructors—Richard Vezzolini, Anita Ullner, Hilary Levine, Stephanie Guerra, Alethea Traskin, Lauren King, and Susan Milos—who welcomed me into their classrooms.

Talks with Bill Marden, Sheryl Loeffler, Lenny Noack, Enrico Cumbo, Bruce Ratcliffe, and Sylvia Robbins provided important inspiration during the initial stages of writing. Later on my brother Tom and his wife Rebecca received chapters as they became available in rough form. Avid and enthusiastic readers, they encouraged me to keep feeding them new pages on a regular basis. Jim Davis was kind enough to read a portion of the manuscript and give me feedback;

Marilyn Harper provided suggestions about how to prepare it for publication.

Steve and Christine Ronsko lived across the street from our family home in Lodi for many years; my family owes them both a lot of thanks for supporting our mother, on a daily basis, during her final years—and for so much more beyond that. Their ongoing interest and encouragement were also crucial in motivating me to complete this project.

About the Author

Steven Roesch was born and raised in Lodi, California. After completing undergraduate studies in German and English at the University of the Pacific in Stockton, he spent two years at the state university in Tübingen before doing graduate work in Comparative Literature at the University of Toronto. His teaching career spanned more than thirty years and included two years of full-time teaching in Germany as part of the Fulbright Interchange Teacher Program. Since his retirement in 2016 Mr. Roesch has devoted his time to teaching online, coaching students in chess at a local elementary school, and completing several translation projects.

Printed in the United States
By Bookmasters